NEGOTIATING FOR SUCCESS:
Essential Strategies and Skills

George Siedel
University of Michigan

Published by Van Rye Publishing, LLC
www.vanryepublishing.com

ISBN-10: 0-9903671-9-3
ISBN-13: 978-0-9903671-9-2

About the Author

George Siedel is the Williamson Family Professor of Business Administration and the Thurnau Professor of Business Law at the University of Michigan. He teaches negotiation in the MBA program at Michigan's Ross School of Business and in seminars around the world to business leaders, entrepreneurs, attorneys, physicians, athletic directors, and judges.

Professor Siedel completed his graduate studies at the University of Michigan and Cambridge University. He has served as a visiting professor at Stanford University and Harvard University and as a Visiting Scholar at University of California, Berkeley. As a Fulbright Scholar, he held a Distinguished Chair in the Humanities and Social Sciences.

Professor Siedel has received several national research awards including the Maurer Award, the Ralph Bunche Award, and the Hoeber Award. He has also received numerous teaching awards, including the 2014 Executive Program Professor of the Year Award from CIMBA, a consortium of thirty-six leading universities committed to international education.

Acknowledgments

Although I am listed as the author, this book is the product of the shared advice, experience and wisdom of literally thousands of students, colleagues, family members, friends, and others. I am unable to mention them all, but listed below is a sampling (in alphabetical order, by last name when individuals are recognized).

I also acknowledge the outstanding research that has improved negotiation theory and practice over the years. Each chapter includes citations to the work of leading negotiation researchers. In an era of powerful search engines, detailed citations (in the form of footnotes that interrupt the flow of text and separate works-cited lists that require constant flipping to the back of a book) are unnecessary. Instead, brief citations are included parenthetically, with enough information to enable readers to easily locate sources by using search engines.

Business Leaders and Professionals. Thank you to the business leaders and professionals from North America, South America, Asia, Africa, Europe, and Australia with whom I have worked over the years. In addition to teaching open seminars, I have offered seminars and given presentations to specific audiences that include pharmaceutical executives, athletic directors, attorneys, physicians, and entrepreneurs. Whether teaching in Seoul, Venice, Sydney, Mumbai, or Sao Paulo, I have learned from these participants that the concepts covered in this book are valuable in all professions, in all cultures and on all continents.

David E. A. Carson. Thank you to David, a successful business leader and prominent alumnus of the Ross School of Business, for establishing the Carson Scholars Program. This program has played a leadership role in providing public policy education to business school undergraduates. As the program's Director, I have had the opportunity to work with distinguished governmental leaders in Washington who, while teaching in the program, shared their insights into behind-the-scenes political negotiations.

Consortium of Universities for International Studies (CIMBA). Thank you to Al Ringleb, Executive Director, and Cristina Turchet, Associate Director, for their innovative leadership of CIMBA and for inviting me to teach an annual negotiation seminar in Italy.

Family. Thank you to my children, Joe, Katie and John, for testing me with various negotiation strategies and tactics when they were young. As is widely known, negotiations with one's children are the toughest form of negotiation. Thanks also to my sister, Karen Braaten, who helped me develop dispute resolution skills when we were youngsters. Happily we have moved beyond dispute resolution and are close friends.

Fulbright International Summer Institute. Thank you to Julia Stefanova, Executive Director of the Fulbright Office in Bulgaria, and to her outstanding staff for providing the opportunity to teach an annual negotiation course there to students from Eastern Europe and beyond.

Helena Haapio. Many thanks to my frequent co-author Helena Haapio, International Contract Counsel for Lexpert Ltd. in Helsinki, Finland, and a leader in the proactive law movement. Helena has been an inspiration in her ability to integrate the theoretical and practical aspects of contracting. Parts of Chapters 8 and 9 in this book are adapted from our book *A Short Guide to Contract Risk* (Gower 2013) and from our 2010 article "Using

Proactive Law for Competitive Advantage," *American Business Law Journal.* I am also grateful to Helena for introducing me to the visualization community. Contract visualization is discussed in Chapter 9.

Harvard Program on Negotiation (PON). Thank you to PON, a leading center for negotiation teaching and research, for providing a warm welcome when I was a Visiting Professor at Harvard Business School and for producing high quality negotiation materials that are used worldwide.

Nancy Hauptman. My thanks to Nancy for her thorough review of the manuscript, for her creative design work on the figures that appear throughout the book, and for her general support and encouragement.

International Association for Contract & Commercial Management (IACCM). Thank you to IACCM and President Tim Cummins. This global association has developed a wealth of resources on best practices relating to contract negotiation and management.

Junhai Liu. Thank you to Junhai, a distinguished professor at Renmin University in Beijing where, at his invitation, I lectured on "Negotiating with Americans." This experience helped me develop the chronological organization used in this book.

Alyssa Martina. Many thanks to Alyssa, a leader and outstanding educator in the field of entrepreneurial negotiation, for her close review of the manuscript and her useful suggestions.

MOOC Students. Thank you to the thousands of students worldwide who have enrolled in my Massive Open Online Course on "Successful Negotiation." This course provided the impetus for completion of this book.

Negotiation Professors. My thanks to professors at leading universities like Harvard, MIT and Stanford for invitations to teach in their negotiation courses and for sharing their insights about negotiation.

Parents. I want to acknowledge my late parents, George and Justine Siedel. While their negotiation skills were forged in difficult times during the Depression, fairness was their highest priority in dealings with others.

Danica Purg. Thank you to Danica, President of IEDC Bled School of Management and President of the international management association CEEMAN, for inviting me to teach negotiation to executives in Slovenia.

Ross School of Business at the University of Michigan. Thank you to the Ross School of Business for the chance to teach negotiation in undergraduate, MBA and executive education programs. I especially appreciated the opportunity to teach an annual negotiation seminar for many years to business executives in Hong Kong and to teach negotiation in Brazil, Korea, India and Thailand. Thank you also to the Ross leadership team for placing trust in me to negotiate the creation of executive education centers in Paris and Hong Kong when I was Associate Dean for Executive Education. These negotiations, along with my negotiations with company leaders to develop executive programs for multinational companies, provided valuable experience in international deal making.

Jeswald Salacuse. Thank you to Jeswald, the Henry J. Braker Professor of Law and former Dean of The Fletcher School at Tufts University, for permission to include the negotiation style assessment tool in Appendix C. Jeswald is recognized as a leader in research and teaching relating to international negotiation.

Acknowledgments

John Siedel. This book would not have been possible without John's technical ability and editorial skills throughout the writing and publication process. His close attention to detail led to many interesting negotiations.

Students. Last, but certainly not least, a special thank you to the undergraduate and MBA students who have taken my negotiation course at the Ross School of Business and beyond. One of the joys in teaching negotiation is the opportunity to continue to learn from diverse, energetic and enthusiastic students.

George Siedel
University of Michigan

Contents

APPENDICES: PLANNING CHECKLIST AND ASSESSMENT TOOL

Introduction

A business executive in my annual negotiation seminar in Italy recently exclaimed: "Life is negotiation!" No one ever stated it better. As a mother with young children and as a company leader, she realized that negotiations are pervasive in our personal and business lives.

We all negotiate on a daily basis. We negotiate with our spouses, children, parents and friends. We negotiate when we rent an apartment, buy a car, purchase a house and apply for a job. The ability to negotiate might be the most important factor in your career advancement.

Negotiation is also the key to business success. No organization can survive without profitable contracts. At a strategic level, businesses are concerned with value creation and achieving competitive advantage. But the success of high-level business strategies depends on contracts made with suppliers, customers and other stakeholders. Contracting capability—the ability to negotiate and perform successful contracts—is the important function in any organization.

My goal in writing this book is to help you achieve success in your personal negotiations and in your business transactions. The book covers the key strategies and skills necessary for negotiation success. Many other books also cover these concepts. However, this book goes beyond concepts by focusing on actions necessary for success.

The book is also unique in its organization by covering each step in the negotiation process chronologically from preparation through performance. This holistic approach avoids a mistaken assumption that success is determined by what happens at the bargaining table. While the "bargaining table" phase of the process is important and is covered in detail in this book, the real test of success is whether the agreement was performed successfully.

By the time you complete this book, you should be able to

- complete a negotiation analysis, that includes your reservation price and zone of potential agreement

- use decision trees to evaluate your alternatives to your negotiation

- assess your negotiating style

- increase your negotiating power

- decide how to resolve ethical dilemmas during negotiations

- use psychological tools—and avoid psychological traps—during negotiations

- evaluate your performance as a negotiator

Beyond these and other specific benefits, I hope that the concepts and tools in this book will help you achieve balance and harmony in your life as you engage in daily personal and business negotiations. Because "life is negotiation!"

I PREPARE TO NEGOTIATE

1 Decide Whether to Negotiate

We all enter into contracts on a daily basis without engaging in negotiation. We usually do not negotiate when we buy food, drink, apps, books, clothing, electronics, pet supplies, office products, household goods, toys and sports equipment. What would happen if we decided to negotiate when purchasing these items?

This is an assignment I give to my students at the University of Michigan. I ask them to try to purchase a personal product or service at a store, hotel or restaurant for less than the listed price. There are two rules. They cannot negotiate for something that is usually bargained for, such as a car or an item at a flea market. And they cannot tell the person with whom they are negotiating that this is a course assignment.

Before they complete the assignment I ask the students to estimate how many of them will be successful. A large percentage of them predict that most students will fail. The actual results are surprising. In a typical year, two-thirds of the students are successful. The discounts range from 1% to 100% and the students save thousands of dollars.

In achieving these savings, students use a variety of strategies and tactics. Some of the strategies—such as a Best Alternative to a Negotiated Agreement (BATNA) strategy, use of stretch goals, and building a relationship with the seller—are based on sound negotiation principles and will be covered later in this book. For example, one student was so successful in establishing a relationship that a checkout clerk offered to lend her money so that she could complete the purchase!

Other tactics fall within the realm of tricks. A student who wanted to purchase a high-priced water bottle tried to project an image of poverty by not shaving, and by wearing shoddy clothing and an old pair of tennis shoes. He also coughed occasionally to indicate that his health was not good. Other students point out defects in products, try to flirt with the other side, or use strategic timing—for instance, by showing up at a pizza store just before closing, realizing that any unsold slices of pizza would be thrown away.

Sometimes students use a combination of tactics. A young father arrived at a sushi restaurant shortly before closing. He put a $20 bill in one pocket and a $10 bill in another so that he could pull out one or the other (depending on how the negotiation proceeded) and claim that this was all the money he had. He also played a sympathy card by emphasizing that his young children at home love sushi. The result was a substantial discount. We will turn to a discussion of ethics in a later chapter!

Even without using tricks or more acceptable strategies, US consumers are discovering that retailers are more willing than ever to haggle. According to an article in the *New York Times* ("More Retailers See Haggling as a Price of Doing Business," December 16, 2013), stores are even training their employees how to negotiate with customers. The article offers this advice to customers: "Pay no attention to the price on that tag."

Three Reasons Why We Don't Haggle More Often

If haggling produces these results, why don't we do it more often? Three reasons come to mind that you should consider when deciding whether to negotiate. First, many people are simply uneasy about negotiating. My students use words such as "hesitant," "embarrassed" and "uncomfortable" when describing their retail negotiating experience. But these feelings are not universal, as other students enjoyed the experience, describing it as "enjoyable," "fun" and "thrilling."

To some students who enjoyed the negotiation, the experience is life-changing, as this student reported: "I felt so good that I went home and began looking for other things . . . to purchase. This activity may have created a monster."

Students in this category often send me emails describing their post-graduation negotiation experiences. For instance, one student reported that the negotiation skills acquired in the course enabled him to save $130 per month on an apartment, although he wasn't able to negotiate a discount on a dessert at a restaurant. A student from Europe was successful in negotiating with the Mafia to obtain the return of her father's car, which had been stolen.

Yet another student reported some good news and bad news. The good news was that he always obtained a discount from hotels. The bad news was that his wife would no longer go with him to the front desk. (A *Wall Street Journal* article, "How Do You Get a Break in the Price of Practically Anything? Easy, Just Ask," August 19, 2006, noted that most hotel desk clerks are authorized to provide discounts ranging from 10% to 25%.)

In addition to discomfort with the process, a second reason why many people don't haggle is that the benefits might not exceed the costs. World-famous negotiation professor Max Bazerman tells this story about himself in his book *Smart Money Decisions* (which is highly recommended). In purchasing a big-screen TV, he completed extensive research on different models and costs. He visited many dealers and obtained quotes that combined the price of the TV with other items like installation and a satellite dish. His efforts over the last twenty hours of his search resulted in savings of around $120. Was this a successful negotiation?

The answer depends on how you want to spend your limited time on earth. Professor Bazerman concluded that he had made a mistake in ignoring the value of his time, which was worth more than $6 an hour. However, if you enjoy negotiating more than the other opportunities that life provides—such as relaxing or spending time with your friends and family—this might be time well-spent.

Before you decide to negotiate instead of enjoying life's other pleasures, consider what Professors Jonah Berger and Aner Sela call "decision quicksand," which is agonizing over trivial decisions such as what brand of dental floss to purchase. (For a summary of their research, see "Research Roundup," *Knowledge@Wharton*, November 7, 2012.)

Although this research focuses on decision making when making purchases, the same trap might apply to decisions whether to negotiate. Do you really want to spend your time negotiating over items that are trivial when compared with the more important issues in life?

The third reason why you might not want to negotiate is that it can carry risks. For example, if an employer makes a job offer, should you negotiate with the employer? In answering this question, you should do a BATNA analysis, as discussed later in this book. You should also be aware of the legal consequences of negotiating. For example, depending on how it is phrased, a counteroffer from you might legally terminate the employer's offer.

Even when your response to the offer is not legally a counteroffer, your attempt at negotiation might cause the employer to withdraw the offer. For example, a college offered a teaching position to a candidate. She responded by asking the college whether it would consider raising the salary and providing other benefits. The college then withdrew the offer of employment. ("Negotiated Out of a Job," *Inside Higher Ed*, March 13, 2014)

Key takeaway. Before beginning a negotiation, ask yourself these questions: Are you comfortable negotiating in this situation? Do benefits from the negotiation outweigh the costs, such as your time commitment? Do the rewards justify the risks, such as losing a job offer?

2   Determine the Type of Negotiation

O nce you have made the decision to negotiate, you should answer three questions before beginning the negotiation analysis described in Chapter 3: Is this a position-based or interest-based negotiation? Does the negotiation involve doing a deal or resolving a dispute? And is this a cross-cultural negotiation?

DECIDE WHETHER THE NEGOTIATION IS POSITION-BASED OR INTEREST-BASED

Traditionally, negotiation was viewed as a position-based activity. For example, you and I are fighting over a gourmet anchovy pizza. My position is that I should get the pizza; your position is that the pizza belongs to you. A friend of ours suggests that I should cut the pizza in half and that you should be able to select the half that you want. Is this a good result?

Over the years I have worked with many business leaders and consultants specializing in negotiation who initially think that this would be a win-win compromise because it seems to be a fair result that satisfies both sides. While true in many situations, it might also be possible to improve the result for both you and me by moving beyond our positions to explore our underlying interests. This is an approach advocated in the classic book on negotiation, *Getting to Yes*, which was originally published in 1981.

For instance, if our friend asked me about my interests—why I want the pizza—I would explain that I hate anchovies but want the crust. Leftover gourmet pizza crusts can be converted into crumbs that are a great addition to vegetable dishes. If she asked why you want the pizza, you might reply that you love anchovy pizza but never eat the crust.

By going beyond positions and identifying underlying interests, we have reached an agreement that benefits each of us without harming the other. When compared with our original solution (cutting the pizza in half), I have doubled the crust I want and you have doubled the anchovy pizza you desire.

Of course, many situations are purely positional—for example, where we both love anchovy pizza and never eat pizza crust. While the search for interests in these situations does no harm, a prolonged search might be a waste of time. So at the outset, you should attempt to identify the type of negotiation. Is it a position-based negotiation (where you divide the pizza) or an interest-based negotiation (where you in effect build a larger pizza).

Conceptually, this seems like a simple question. However, the question becomes complicated because negotiation experts use a variety of terms to describe these two alternatives. For example, academics often refer to dividing the pizza as "distributive" negotiation because it involves distributing the pieces of a fixed-sized pie, while enlarging the pizza is called "integrative" negotiation because the goal is to expand the pizza by integrating the parties' interests.

Other experts refer to dividing the pizza as claiming value (you want to get the largest possible piece of a fixed-sized pie) and expanding the pizza as creating value (by building a larger pizza). The latter approach, value creation, is a key business goal. While discussed in corporate board rooms at a strategic and conceptual level, the reality is that value creation takes place on a day-to-day basis during business negotiations throughout the company. Companies that have developed negotiation expertise have a strong source of advantage over their competitors.

Other terms used to describe negotiations that focus on dividing the pie include competitive, win/lose, zero sum, and adversarial. Negotiations that attempt to enlarge the pizza are described as cooperative, win/win, non-zero-sum, and problem-solving.

When I teach negotiation around the world and emphasize the importance of attempting to enlarge the pizza by searching for underlying interests, I am often challenged by people with extensive business experience. They contend that most negotiations are position-based rather than interest-based. When you sell your product to a customer you lock into a position—high price— and the buyer locks into another position—low price. If you are negotiating with a car dealer, the dealer wants a high price and you want to pay a low price.

On the other hand, many experienced negotiators are enthusiastic about interest-based negotiation. So which side is correct?

In my opinion, both sides are correct. In a typical negotiation two sides each start with a position—high price vs. low price, for example. They should then always search for underlying interests by asking the "why" question in an attempt to identify any underlying interests. Why do you want the pizza?

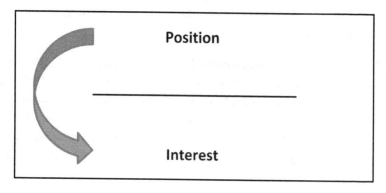

This questioning will result in two possibilities. First, the parties might discover that there are no underlying interests they can use to build a larger pie. In this case they revert to positional negotiation. Second, they might identify interests that enable them to build a larger pie. In this situation they also revert to positional bargaining as they then negotiate over their respective shares of the larger pie.

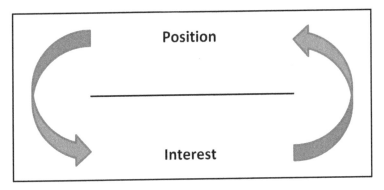

Key takeaway. Once you decide to negotiate, you should first attempt to decide whether the negotiation is position-based or interest-based. Even when you think it is a position-based negotiation, you should attempt to search for underlying interests. If you are unable to find those interests your negotiation is positional. But even if you identify underlying interests and build a larger pie, your negotiation still becomes positional—though now there is an opportunity for both sides to obtain larger pieces because the pie is bigger.

DECIDE WHETHER THE NEGOTIATION INVOLVES DOING A DEAL OR RESOLVING A DISPUTE

The second question you should address after deciding to negotiate is whether the negotiation involves doing a deal or resolving a dispute. In an article titled "The Janus Quality of Negotiation:

Dealmaking and Dispute Settlement" (*Negotiation Journal*, April, 1988), Frank Sander and Jeffrey Rubin summarize the difference between the two types of negotiation by reference to the Roman god Janus. Janus has two faces, one looking to the future and one to the past.

Like the right side of Janus, deal-making negotiation looks to the future. The emphasis is on problem solving and on identifying the parties' interests. Dispute resolution negotiation, like the left side of Janus tends to look to the past, with a focus on positions and on claiming value in an adversarial manner.

While the difference between deal-making and dispute-resolution negotiations will affect your negotiation strategy, even dispute resolution can be converted into an interest-based negotiation. I give my students a real-life scenario involving a dispute between a company that developed a statistical software package and its licensee. The company learned that the licensee was working on an adaptation of the software, which the licensee planned to market to other companies in violation of the licensing agreement. The company sued the licensee for several million dollars.

In analyzing this situation from the perspective of the software company, most students become adversarial and position-based. They conclude that they have a strong case and recommend against settlement of the lawsuit. But a few students recognize that both sides can benefit by working together to form a joint venture. Rather than letting the court determine who wins and who loses, which is a "zero sum game," they both can win through a strategic marketing plan that increases total profits that exceed the sum of their separate profits.

Key takeaway. Whenever possible, try to convert a dispute-resolution negotiation into a deal-making negotiation by searching for underlying interests that can be integrated to benefit both sides.

Types of Dispute-Resolution Processes

When you cannot settle a dispute through negotiation, several other dispute resolution processes are available. A dispute on my campus (as reported in *The Michigan Daily*) illustrates these processes. At 4:00 a.m. on a cold February morning, a line of students began to form outside the basketball arena. The students wanted to purchase tickets for a game that would be played later that day.

At 7:00 a.m. another line began to form in a different location. Students in this line claimed that the other students were waiting in the wrong location and demanded that they move to the back of the other (7:00 a.m.) line. This caused a dispute that needed resolution. In a simple dispute like this or in more complex business disputes, several processes can be used in addition to negotiation.

Avoidance. As the name implies, resolution can result when one party avoids the dispute by conceding to the other side.

Mediation. Mediation is much like negotiation except that a third party, the mediator, assists the parties in resolving the dispute. Think of mediation as assisted negotiation.

Arbitration. Arbitration also involves a third party but, unlike mediation, the third party—the arbitrator—has authority to reach a decision in the dispute. Under the typical arbitration process, the disputing parties must abide by the decision.

Litigation. As with arbitration, the third party—the judge—has authority to reach a decision. Unlike arbitration, the proceedings are public.

Power. Parties in a powerful position can force the other side to do they want.

In the ticket line dispute several processes were used. First, the police arrived and, acting as arbitrators, decided that the students in the 4:00 a.m. line were in the wrong place and ordered them to move to the rear of the 7:00 a.m. line. Second, a representative of the athletic department acted as a mediator and arranged for all students to obtain tickets. Third, at a meeting the following morning, the students entered into negotiations to prevent this type of dispute from arising in the future.

Perspectives on Dispute Resolution Processes

Regardless of whether you are involved in a personal dispute or a business dispute, you should consider a variety of perspectives when selecting a dispute-resolution process.

Alternative dispute resolution perspective. In business disputes, litigation is often viewed as the enemy because it results in substantial costs in terms of time and money. Several years ago, business leaders began to question why they were outsourcing business disputes to lawyers and the court system. One of these leaders, CEO Walter Wriston of Citicorp, invited representatives from ten business schools to a meeting in New York City, where he emphasized to us the importance of courses on alternatives to litigation.

This meeting encouraged business schools to offer courses on alternative dispute resolution (ADR) processes: arbitration, mediation and negotiation. Understanding these processes is important because business negotiations often include discussion of ADR procedures that will be used if problems arise in performing a contract. ADR will be covered in greater detail in Chapter 10.

Attorneys, by the way, have mixed emotions about ADR. Some commentators have joked that within law firms ADR stands for "alarming drop in revenue." However, many leading firms have embraced ADR and have developed expertise in using ADR processes.

Third-party processes. Third-party processes—litigation, arbitration and mediation—are important to business leaders for two reasons. First, they use third party processes in resolving disputes with other businesses. Second, in their day-to-day work within their companies, leaders use these processes when acting as third parties in resolving disputes between their subordinates.

Power, rights and interests. Academics often use a power, rights and interests framework when describing negotiation and other dispute-resolution processes. Power was mentioned earlier. The rights-oriented processes are litigation and arbitration, where the third party decides who is right and who is wrong. The interests-oriented processes are mediation and negotiation.

Although academic in origin, the power/rights/interests framework provides a useful tool for managers faced with a dispute. The following list, paraphrased from a major corporation's internal document, illustrates a manager's options in the event of a dispute:

1. *Power.* Use power to force the other side to meet our demands.

2. *Rights.* Allow a judge or arbitrator to decide whether we are right.

3. *Avoidance.* Give in to the other side.

4. *Interests.* Negotiate an agreement based on our underly-

ing interests.

For example, if your company is involved in a dispute with a supplier and several other suppliers want your business, you might want to use the power option to force the supplier to do what you want. On the other hand, if your dispute is with key customers, you might use the avoidance option and let them have what they want, even if you are certain that you are right.

Using dispute-resolution processes in deal making. Historically, negotiation has been the key process for doing deals, while all the processes described previously are used for dispute resolution. However, in recent years negotiators have started to use dispute-resolution processes such as arbitration and mediation when doing deals. This shift will be described in Chapter 10.

Key takeaway. Try to convert dispute resolution into a deal-making negotiation by searching for underlying interests. Consider using ADR and power/rights/interests perspectives when attempting to resolve disputes. Also try to use dispute resolution processes like mediation and arbitration when doing deals.

DECIDE WHETHER YOU ARE INVOLVED IN A CROSS-CULTURAL NEGOTIATION

A cross-cultural negotiation involves unique challenges, the first of which is determining whether you are in one! We often think that cross-cultural negotiations involve parties from different countries—for example, a negotiation between parties from Brazil and India. However, because many countries are multicultural, you might become involved in a cross-cultural negotiation with your next-door neighbor.

In a typical negotiation, you first analyze your own interests and also the interests of the other side. Then during the negotiation you attempt to determine whether your perception of the other side's interests is accurate.

Cross-cultural negotiations, however, raise two hurdles that you must leap in determining your counterpart's interests. The first hurdle is the negotiating style of the other side, also known as the "surface culture." The other hurdle is understanding the values and beliefs of the other side, often called the "deep culture." (Ball & McCulloch, *International Business*)

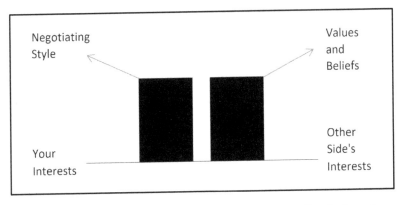

A major challenge in surmounting these two hurdles is that there often are variations within a culture. For example, when I served as Associate Dean of the Ross School of Business at the University of Michigan, one of my responsibilities was a program in which we sent MBA students to the Navajo reservation. Before my first visit to the reservation, I tried to learn about Navajo culture by reading books and reviewing websites. I discovered, for example, that in the Navajo culture handshakes are weak and it is impolite to look someone directly in the eye.

Upon arriving at the reservation, the first Navajo I met looked me straight in the eye and gave me a firm handshake. While I felt foolish looking off to the side and offering a limp hand, I later learned that his actions were unusual. But this provided a memorable lesson that there are variations within a culture and stereotyping should be avoided.

Jeswald Salacuse, former Dean at The Fletcher School at Tufts University and a leading expert on international negotiation, has developed an assessment for cross-cultural negotiations that involves a three-step process. First, complete the assessment, which is at Appendix C in the Appendices. Second, estimate where your counterpart from the other culture falls along the spectrum for each item on the list. Third, do a gap analysis: Where are the major gaps between your and the other side's negotiating styles? This will focus your preparations for the cross-cultural negotiation.

Completing the assessment and gap analysis is a useful exercise even when you aren't involved in a cross-cultural negotiation. But when preparing for a cross-cultural negotiation, a fourth step is advisable. After you have identified the gaps, you should practice for an upcoming negotiation with a role reversal exercise, where you adopt the style of the other culture.

This exercise has two benefits. First, it provides a deeper under-standing of the other side's style that will be useful during your negotiation. Second, this exercise might provide tactics that you can try in the future.

For example, I often assign a role reversal where some of my students are limited in what they can say during a negotiation. They later report that this exercise enables them to understand the power of silence. For instance, when they remain silent, the other side will often continue to talk, revealing useful information about their interests and BATNA (a concept we will cover in Chapter 3). They also discover that when they say little, the other side listens more closely to what they say.

One last question to consider when preparing for a cross-cultural negotiation relates to an old adage: "When in Rome, do as the Romans do." Is this good advice for negotiators? When you are negotiating in another culture, should you adopt the local negotiating style?

Answering "yes" to these questions can cause two problems. First, if the other side adopts the same approach, you both might feel silly trying to use each other's style. Someone told me about a picture of a Japanese negotiator meeting an American negotiator for the first time. The Japanese negotiator reached out to hug the American just as the American bowed, resulting in an air hug.

The second problem is that if you don't fully understand the other culture, your attempts to mimic the other side's style might be considered offensive. One of the participants in my negotiation seminar for executives was the CEO of a foreign subsidiary of a major multinational corporation. Unlike other expatriates, who often live in enclaves with other company executives from their home country, he moved his family to a small village and thoroughly immersed himself into the local culture. Because of this experience he felt confident adopting the negotiating style—but he was the exception.

The best advice I have ever received on the "when in Rome" question came from a former student of mine from Japan who rose to the top level of the largest life insurance company in the world. When I asked him whether Americans should adopt a Japanese style when negotiating in Japan, he replied:

> Americans should stay with their own style. Of course, it is important to respect the culture of each country. If we respect each other, the negotiation will be comfortable and constructive. When I negotiated with people from the US, including Jim Robinson (former CEO of American Express) and Richard Fuld (former CEO of Lehman Brothers), or the people of Europe, including Dr. Breuer (CEO of Deutsche Bank), I felt very comfortable about their style, although they were more straightforward, more open, more aggressive, and their attitude was more

relaxed, especially the Americans. The success of negotiation between cross-national companies depends on
respect of each other rather than style.

Key takeaway. Do a gap analysis to understand how your negotiation style differs from your counterpart's style. Keep in mind that
there are variations within each culture. Conduct research so that
you can avoid conduct that is offensive in other cultures, but be
cautious in attempting to adopt the negotiation style of another
culture.

3   Conduct a Negotiation Analysis

Once you have determined the type of negotiation you are involved in (interest-based vs. position-based? deal-making vs. dispute resolution? cross-cultural?), you are ready to conduct a negotiation analysis. In this chapter we first explore the general questions you should ask when completing the analysis. We then focus on two specific aspects of your analysis—your Best Alternative to a Negotiated Agreement (BATNA) considerations when you are involved in a dispute resolution negotiation and the use of decisions trees to calculate your BATNA.

Ask Six Questions When Conducting a Negotiation Analysis

Let's assume that you are engaged in a simple, everyday negotiation—the sale of a car. You are preparing to negotiate with a potential buyer, Kyle. Kyle is the only person who responded to your sales ad. You need at least $4,000 from the sale of the car to finance the purchase of a truck you have ordered.

You want to keep your car for three more weeks, which is when the truck will arrive. The reasonable value of the car (based on several online calculators) is $5,000. If you can't find a buyer willing to pay at least $4,500, you will sell the car to your friend Terry for $4,000. You know that Terry will let you keep the car for the next three weeks.

When I ask participants in my negotiation seminars about their analysis and strategy going into a negotiation like this (or a more complex business negotiation), I often receive vague responses that focus on asking the other side questions. Questioning is an important tactic that we will explore in Chapter 5. However, the benefits of questioning are diluted if you do not have benchmarks in mind that will enable you to evaluate the answers you receive. In the words of retired baseball player Yogi Berra, "If you don't know where you are going, you'll end up someplace else." Here is a checklist of six questions you should ask yourself to help you understand where you want to go.

1. **What is my overall goal in the negotiation? Why is this your goal?** In this situation, your goal is to sell your car. You want to sell the car so that you can finance the purchase of a truck that is on order.

2. **What issues are most important to me in reaching this goal and why are these issues important?** Chapter 2 emphasized the importance of moving beyond what you want (your position) and asking why you want it (your interests). In this case, the key issues (and interests) are price (so that you can finance the purchase of the truck) and transfer date (because you need the car for the next three weeks while you await delivery of your truck).

3. **What is my Best Alternative to a Negotiated Agreement (BATNA)?** This acronym entered the realm of negotiation analysis in 1981 with the publication of the book *Getting to Yes*. Stated another way, what is your best alternative if there is no deal? Identifying your best alternative is especially important because this is what gives you leverage in a negotiation. With a strong alternative you are more powerful in the negotiation. In the words of one of my students, you should "fall in love" with your BATNA—if it is strong!

   In this case, your best alternative is to sell the car to your friend Terry for $4,000. Your willingness to accept a lower price from Terry than the minimum amount ($4,500) you would require from Kyle illustrates the importance of relationships in negotiations. When there is a strong relationship negotiators are often more flexible in their demands.

4. **What is my reservation price?** This is the highest price a buyer is willing to pay or the lowest price a seller is willing to take. In this negotiation your reservation price is $4,500.

5. **What is the most likely price?** In this negotiation the facts indicate that the reasonable value of the car is $5,000.

6. **What is my stretch goal?** This important concept is also the fuzziest part of the analysis. Your stretch goal in a negotiation like this is a number that is higher than the most likely price from the seller's perspective and lower than the most likely price from the buyer's perspective.

    Generally, negotiators who set the most ambitious stretch goals are the most successful in negotiations, with one important caveat. If you have no factual basis for your stretch goal, you risk losing credibility with the other side.

    For example, in 1997 boxer Mike Tyson bought a 56,000 square foot house with 18 bedrooms and 38 bathrooms for $2.7 million. The following year, he tried to sell the house and set an ambitious stretch goal of $22 million. When there were no takers he eventually lowered the asking price to $5 million before taking the house off the market. Apparently, he had lost credibility. This story was reported in a *Wall Street Journal* article entitled "No Bites on Tyson House" (January 25, 2002).

Apart from the risk of losing credibility, there are no firm guidelines on setting stretch goals. Let's assume here that your stretch goal is $6,000.

In answering these questions, it often helps to visualize your conclusions.

	Reservation Price	Most Likely	Stretch
BATNA			
	4500	5000	6000

As we will discuss in Chapter 7 when looking at the psychology of negotiation, great negotiators have the ability to look at a negotiation from the perspective of the other side. So when preparing for negotiation you should try to estimate Kyle's answers to these questions.

Of course, these numbers will not be precise and you will try to obtain additional information after negotiations begin. But for the time being, let's assume that Kyle's reservation price (that is, the most that Kyle will pay) is $5,500, the most likely price estimate is $4,500 and the stretch goal is $3,500. We can also assume that Kyle's BATNA is to purchase a car from someone else.

	Reservation Price	Most Likely	Stretch
BATNA			
	4500	5000	6000
3500	4500	5500	
			BATNA
Stretch	Most Likely	Reservation Price	

With these figures in mind, you are now ready to complete the last part of the analysis—calculation of the Zone of Potential Agreement or ZOPA. This is the zone in which the deal can take place. In this case the price will be no lower than your reservation price, $4500, and no higher than Kyle's reservation price, $5500. Here is a depiction of the analysis from both sides.

	Reservation Price	Most Likely	Stretch
BATNA			
	4500	5000	6000

Zone of Potential Agreement (ZOPA)

3500	4500	5500	
			BATNA
Stretch	Most Likely	Reservation Price	

As an aside, when some Russian students took my course in Bulgaria a few years ago they started to laugh whenever I referred to ZOPA. For instance, I mentioned that it's great to walk into a negotiation with a large ZOPA. When I asked them what was funny about ZOPAs I was advised that this is a Russian word for one's posterior. Language variations are a challenge when teaching in a cross-cultural setting!

This particular negotiation analysis has focused on price. But how should you analyze the other main issue that is important to you—your goal of keeping the car for three more weeks? You should try to anticipate Kyle's response to this request.

There are two possible responses. First, Kyle might not care about the transfer date. As a shrewd negotiator Kyle might feign interest in order to lower the price, but at least you will be able to work out a deal.

The more challenging response might be that Kyle needs the car immediately, so that your two positions are directly in conflict. You should prepare for this possibility by moving beyond Kyle's position—"I need the car immediately"—to explore underlying interests.

For instance, when you ask Kyle the "why" question ("Why do you need the car immediately?"), the response might be that Kyle needs the car to travel to work. You might then be able to figure out a way to meet this need by providing alternative transportation over the next three weeks. You might even offer to drive Kyle to work.

Key takeaway. Prepare for negotiations by asking yourself the six questions described in this chapter and try to predict how the other side will answer these questions. Also be prepared to search for underlying interests.

Your BATNA Analysis in a Dispute Resolution Negotiation

As noted earlier, BATNA is a key concept because it gives you leverage in a negotiation. In most business transactions, application of the concept is fairly straightforward because it involves considering alternative deals. The concept becomes more complicated in dispute-resolution negotiations, where the BATNA ultimately might be a court proceeding.

The dispute-resolution scenario requires a basic understanding of, first, the litigation process and, second, techniques for evaluating litigation outcomes. This section will review the litigation process and the next section will discuss a tool for evaluating outcomes in both deal-making and dispute-resolution negotiations.

This explanation of the litigation process will examine fundamental differences between litigation in the United States and other countries. In a global economy it is especially important for you to understand these differences so that you can make sound decisions regarding litigation strategy and settlement possibilities. Here are five key differences.

1. **Contingency fees.** In the United States, attorneys are hired on a contingency fee basis, which means that their fees are contingent on the outcome of the case. For example, if a lawyer hired on a 30% contingency fee basis wins $10 million, the fee would be $3 million. If the lawyer loses the case, the fee would be 30% of zero. In recent years the contingency fee system has spread to several countries beyond the United States.

2. **Punitive damages.** In countries around the world the purpose of damages is to compensate a party injured by someone else. But in certain circumstances courts in the US will award punitive damages designed to punish someone whose actions were intentional, malicious, or reckless.

3. **Discovery.** Discovery is the process by which lawyers uncover evidence that is used in litigation. Courts in the US have historically been more liberal in allowing lawyers to search for evidence by rummaging through documents held by the opposing party.

4. **Juries.** In the US, unlike most countries, juries are allowed to decide civil cases.

5. **"American Rule."** In the US the traditional rule is that each side must pay its own attorney's fees, even after winning the case. Other countries have a "Loser Pays" rule (also known as the "Everywhere but America Rule"), where the losing party must pay the winner's legal fees.

In combination, these features of the US system can make litigation an attractive BATNA for plaintiffs. For example, if I hire an attorney on a contingency fee basis to sue you, you would hire your own attorney to defend the case. If the court dismisses the lawsuit I would owe my attorney nothing because the fee would be contingent on a successful outcome. And under the American Rule I would not have to cover your attorney fees even though I am the losing party.

To illustrate these five elements in the US system let's examine a case decided by the Tennessee Supreme Court, *Flax v. DaimlerChrysler* (272 S.W.3d 521). In this case a grandfather drove a Dodge Caravan with three passengers—a friend who was sitting in the front seat, the driver's daughter in the seat behind her father, and his 8-month-old grandson in the seat behind the passenger. Someone driving a pickup truck well over the speed limit crashed into the rear end of the Caravan, causing the passenger's seatback to collapse onto the baby, who died from his injuries.

Though not discussed in the case, we can assume that negotiations between the car company and the parents over damages were not successful and the case proceeded to the BATNA—a court decision. We can also assume that the parents hired an attorney on a **contingency fee** basis, though this was not discussed in the case.

Cases begin with the filing of a complaint. In their complaint, the baby's parents alleged that the seats were defective and that the company failed to warn consumers. In answering the complaint the company denied that the seats were defective.

The next stage after the complaint and answer is **discovery**. In this case, the parents' attorney discovered that the company's Safety Leadership Team had concluded "that the seats were inadequate to protect consumers." The company had ordered destruction of minutes from a meeting where this issue was discussed, disbanded the team and fired the team chair.

The next stage is the trial, where a **jury** awarded the parents $5 million in damages for the wrongful death of their baby and another $98 million in **punitive damages**. The trial and appellate courts eventually reduced the punitive damages to $13.4 million, so the damages ultimately totaled $18.4 million. Though not discussed by the court, we can assume that under the **American Rule**, the parents' attorney fees were deducted from this total and were not recoverable from the company.

One feature that the US system unfortunately shares with other legal systems is that the process takes a long time. The accident in this case took place on June 30, 2001; the final decision in the case was reached almost eight years later on May 26, 2009.

Key takeaway. When you negotiate the settlement of a dispute, your ultimate BATNA might be litigation. This BATNA is often not attractive, especially in the United States, which should encourage you to attempt to reach a negotiated agreement.

Use Decision Trees to Calculate Your BATNA

This section describes decision trees, which are valuable tools that can be used to calculate your BATNA in both deal-making and dispute-resolution negotiations. This tool is also useful in making other types of personal decisions (should I undergo knee surgery?) and business decisions (should I invest in a risky venture?).

Calculate your dispute-resolution BATNA. Let's first look at the use of a decision tree to calculate the value of your ultimate BATNA in a dispute-resolution negotiation—a trial. Suppose that your company has sued a supplier for $4.6 million. Your attorney advises you that there is a 50-50 chance that your company will win. Future legal expenses to litigate the case total $400,000.

During negotiations the supplier offers to settle the case for $2 million. Should you accept the offer? As in any negotiation your answer will depend on your BATNA. While your emotions and attitude toward risk might come into play, let's examine how a decision tree can be used for a logical calculation of the value of your BATNA.

The first step in a decision tree analysis is to depict the decision as a tree on its side. A square or rectangle represents the decision and circles depict uncertainties. This step in the process is useful in clarifying your thinking even if you stop here.

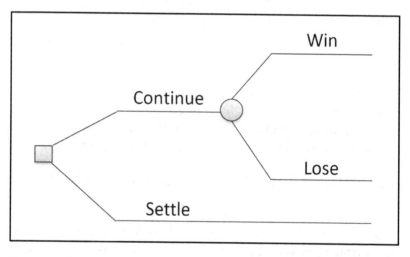

Step two in the process is to add numbers to the tree. The 50-50 chance of winning is shown at the uncertainty node and the financial consequences are shown at the endpoints of each branch. Legal expenses have been deducted to arrive at the $4.2 million figure.

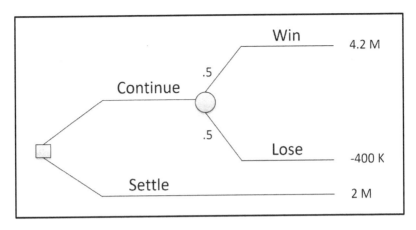

Finally, the expected value of continuing with the litigation is determined by calculating a weighted average of the two uncertain possibilities. Fifty percent of 4.2 plus 50% of negative $400,000 totals $1.9 million. This is less than the settlement offer of $2 million, so logic would tell you to accept the offer because it is better than your BATNA (continuing with the litigation).

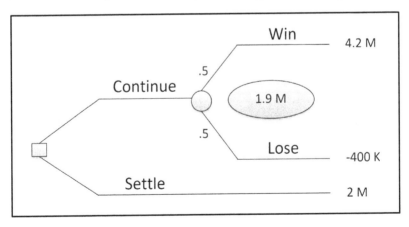

Calculate your deal-making BATNA. The same process can be used to calculate your BATNA when you are doing a deal. Let's say you are negotiating to acquire Company A, which is valued at $21 million. If you purchase A, there is a 90% chance the government will challenge the acquisition and a 60% chance the government will win. If the government wins, the value of A will drop to $14 million because of legal fees and sell-off costs. Even if the government loses, the value of A will drop to $19 million because of legal fees.

Your BATNA is to acquire Company B. B is valued at $15 million and is available for the same price as A. You are certain that the government will not challenge the acquisition of B. Would you proceed with the purchase of A or would you focus on your BATNA—the purchase of B?

A decision tree analysis follows the same steps described earlier. You start with a picture of the decision that looks like a tree on its side. In this case, however, there are two uncertainties branching off from a decision to acquire A: (1) whether the government will challenge the acquisition and, if so, (2) whether the government will win.

After drawing the tree you then assign probabilities—the 90% chance that the government will challenge the acquisition and 60% chance that the government will win. You would also add the financial consequences at the end of each branch of the decision tree.

Finally, you calculate the weighted averages to come up with an expected value of $16.5 million if you acquire A. Logic would tell you to proceed with the acquisition of A because this value is higher than the $15 million value of your BATNA (the acquisition of B).

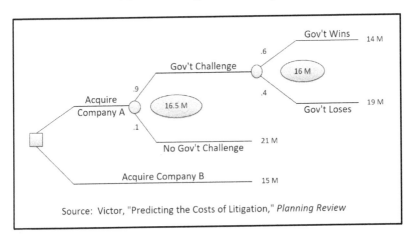

Source: Victor, "Predicting the Costs of Litigation," *Planning Review*

Key takeaway. Decision trees are valuable tools for calculating your BATNA in both dispute-resolution and deal-making negotiations. This tool is also useful for making a variety of other personal and business decisions.

4 Decide How to Answer Ethical Questions

No other human activity tests your ethical standards as much as negotiation. Ethical decision making is sometimes treated by negotiation teachers and authors as a "squishy" subject with no definite standards. In fact, there are guidelines that you should have clearly in mind before beginning any negotiation.

This chapter will focus first on guidelines provided by the law when you face ethical dilemmas during negotiations and will then move beyond the law to examine general ethical standards.

Use Law-Based Ethical Standards

To conceptualize the relationship between law and ethics, visualize two overlapping circles. The circle on the left represents legal principles and the circle on the right represents ethical principles.

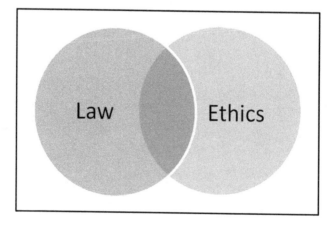

The section of the legal circle that does not intersect the ethical circle represents legal rules that have little or nothing to do with ethics. For example, the law in some countries requires you to drive on the right-hand side of the road and in other countries on the left-hand side. This is simply a legal rule of convenience that is unrelated to ethical considerations.

The section of the ethics circle that does not intersect the legal circle represents situations where the law does not provide guidance for the ethical dilemmas you will face. If you notice that a toddler has fallen into a pool, the law (at least in the United States) does not require you to rescue the child. You would have to rely on ethical standards in deciding how to act.

The overlap between the circles represents areas where legal rules are closely related to ethical principles. "Thou shalt not kill" is an ethical standard as well as a legal rule. Three law-based ethical standards in this overlap area are especially useful when you face ethical dilemmas during negotiations: fraud, fiduciary duty and unconscionability.

Fraud. Fraud is defined as a false representation of a material fact that is relied on by the other side. In other words, it is illegal to lie about facts that the other side relies on during negotiations.

The false representation must relate to a fact that goes beyond puffery, the subjective boasting that is common in advertising. For example, according to an article in *USA Today* (February 26, 2014) a group of consumers sued cyclist Lance Armstrong arguing that he committed fraud by claiming that certain energy products were his "secret weapon" leading to his success. They claimed that he lied because his real secret weapon was doping. A Los Angeles judge dismissed the case after concluding that Armstrong's statements were puffery.

Sometimes even statements that are technically true can be considered fraudulent if they need clarification. For example, a couple in Washington was interested in purchasing a hotel. During negotiations the owner gave them information about the monthly income.

After completing the purchase they learned that the hotel was being run as a house of prostitution and the monthly income was based on this activity. The court in *Ikeda v. Curtis* (261 P.2d 684) allowed them to recover damages, noting that:

> A representation literally true is actionable if used to create an impression substantially false. In the case at bar there was no misrepresentation as to the amount of the income .... [The owner] deceived them to their damage by failing to reveal the source of the income.

There are two areas where the temptation to tell deliberate lies is especially strong during negotiations. First, suppose that I am negotiating to purchase your house. You have offered the house for $300,000. During negotiations I ask you whether you will take $250,000 for the house. You respond "absolutely not," when in fact you would take any amount above $240,000. In other words, you are bluffing about your reservation price of $240,000.

Is your deliberate lie about the reservation price fraudulent? Probably not. This type of bluffing is part of the negotiation game that the other side should expect. To use wording from the above definition of fraud, your statement should not be considered a "material fact that is relied on by the other side." As noted in commentary to the Model Rules of Professional Conduct for attorneys,

> Under generally accepted conventions in negotiation, certain types of statements ordinarily are not taken as statements of material fact. Estimates of price or value placed on the subject of a transaction and a party's intentions as to an acceptable settlement of a claim are ordinarily in this category ....

Although the law might allow you to play the negotiation game in these circumstances, you should still consider the general ethical standards discussed later in this chapter. You should also realize that even the law has limits on how far you can play the negotiation game.

For example, in negotiating the sale of the house to me, what if you tell another lie by stating that other buyers are willing to pay the $300,000 that you are requesting, when in fact there are no other buyers. In other words, you are lying to me about your BATNA. In this scenario there is precedent for holding you liable if I proceed to purchase your house in reliance on this lie.

Fiduciary duty. A fiduciary duty is the highest duty of trust and loyalty, the type of duty that agents (including employees) owe their principals. Suppose, for example, that a real estate developer hires you to obtain a $10 million loan commitment from a financial institution. The developer promises you a commission of $50,000. You successfully obtain the commitment and the financial institution is so pleased with the deal that it pays you a finder's fee.

If the developer refuses to pay, are you entitled to the $50,000 commission? No, said a Georgia court in *Spratlin v. Hawn* (156 S.E.2d 402). The agent in that case violated the fiduciary duty owed to the developer by accepting the finder's fee. An agent cannot "compromise himself by attempting to serve two masters having a contrary interest . . . ." In this situation, the agent should have disclosed the dual agency to both principals.

Unconscionability. Unconscionability is one of the most awkward words in the English language; when you type it, you will receive a flag for misspelling. However, it is an important concept in negotiations that occurs when there is a power imbalance between the parties. In essence, the law requires you to act morally when you are the more powerful party.

Courts focus on two issues in deciding whether a contract is unconscionable. First, they look at the negotiation process (procedural unconscionability): Was the weaker party forced to accept the contract terms because of unequal bargaining power? Second, they look at the substance of the deal (substantive unconscionability): Are the terms of the deal so unreasonable that they violate principles of good conscience?

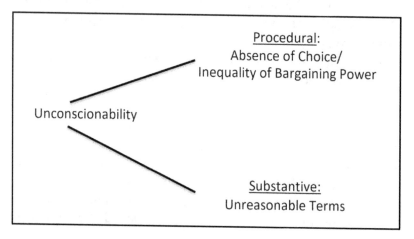

An example of unconscionability involved the restaurant Hooters, which had adopted an alternative dispute resolution program. As part of the program, employees had to sign an "Agreement to arbitrate employment-related disputes," in which they agreed to arbitrate all employment disputes, including sexual harassment claims. A bartender at Hooters who signed the agreement filed suit in federal court claiming sexual harassment.

When Hooters argued that she had to use arbitration instead of going to court, the trial court concluded that the arbitration agreement was unconscionable and an appellate court agreed, noting that the rules in the arbitration agreement were "so one-sided that their only possible purpose is to undermine the neutrality of the proceeding."

Among the reasons for this decision: Arbitrators were selected from a list created by Hooters. Hooters could cancel the agreement to arbitrate, but employees could not. And Hooters could change the rules of the arbitration at any time. (*Hooters v. Phillips*, 173 F.3d 933)

Even when your negotiations are not legally unconscionable, there are other reasons for caution in exercising power when negotiations are one-sided. One reason is summarized in a popular J. Paul Getty quote: "My father said: you must never try to make all the money that's in a deal. Let the other fellow make some money too, because if you have a reputation for always making all the money, you won't have many deals."

Another reason for caution is that the power balance might shift in the future. A senior executive in one of my courses worked for a company that signed over $100 million in contracts with trucking companies that shipped its products. During a time when the economy was weak and there was excess shipping capacity, the company had played tough in negotiating very low shipping rates. When the contracts terminated three years later, it was the truckers' turn to play hardball because by that time the economy had improved and they had developed strong BATNAs.

Use General Ethical Standards Beyond the Law

When legal guidelines are not helpful, a menu of ethical standards is available to help you resolve the ethical dilemmas that arise during negotiations. Here are some examples.

Organizational standards. If your ethical dilemma arises at work, you should look to your company's code of conduct for guidance. As Lynn Paine, a professor at Harvard Business School, has observed, your company standards might have a compliance focus, where the goal is to prevent liability by complying with the law. Or the company might have an integrity focus, where the goal is to encourage responsible conduct through standards that go beyond the law. ("Managing for Organizational

Integrity," *Harvard Business Review*) Or the company might combine the two strategies.

An example of an integrity focus arose in 1982, when Johnson & Johnson faced a major dilemma. Seven people died from cyanide poisoning after taking the company's Tylenol product:

- 12-year-old girl

- 27-year-old postal worker, his brother and sister-in-law

- 27-year-old mother (recovering from birth of son)

- 35-year-old flight attendant

- 31-year-old office worker

Someone had added the poison to Tylenol by tampering with bottles in a store. The police were never able to find the criminal.

Tylenol was an important product for the company, producing 15% of its profits. Over a four-day period that involved intense negotiations over how to handle the situation, the company considered recalling the product, as well as 150 other possible courses of action. In making a final decision, the company turned to its credo: "We believe our first responsibility is to the doctors, nurses and patients, to mothers and fathers and all others who use our products and services."

With this credo in mind, the decision became much simpler: Recall the product. Around 31 million bottles were recalled nationally, resulting in a $100 million loss. During the month following the recall the company developed triple-seal packaging and within two years had regained most of its market share.

Someone you admire. When confronted with an ethical concern, think of someone you admire and ask yourself what that person would do to resolve the dilemma. This could be someone you read about—perhaps an historical figure—or someone you observe at work.

A Qualcomm attorney explained why he admired CEO Irwin Jacobs. During negotiations, the other side accidentally sent the attorney a fax that appeared to provide confidential information about the negotiations. As he tells the story, "I ran into Irwin's office with the fax. But before I could even start to read it, he asked, 'Was it meant to go to us?' When I told him it wasn't, he said, 'Send it back.' I left with my tail between my legs. He's a very ethical person. Most people would have read that document." (*National Law Journal*, January 31, 2000)

Family and newspaper tests. Would you feel comfortable telling your family about your actions during a negotiation? How would you feel when reading about your actions on the front page of the local newspaper? Sometimes these two tests are combined. As legendary investor Warren Buffett put it: "After they first obey all rules, I then want employees to ask themselves whether they are willing to have any contemplated act appear the next day on the front page of their local paper, to be read by their spouses, children, and friends."

Golden Rule. The Golden Rule is part of every major religion in the world. Although the precise wording differs, the rule basically suggests that you should treat others as you want to be treated.

This rule is closely aligned with notions of fairness. In my negotiation course I sometimes conduct what is called an ultimatum game. (Guth, et al., "An Experimental Analysis of Ultimatum Bargaining," *Journal of Economic Behavior and Organization*) Each person on one side of the classroom (the "Allocators") receives an imaginary $1000, which they are to split with someone on the other side of the room (the "Recipients").

The Allocators determine how the money is to be split. For

example, an Allocator might take $999 and give the Recipient $1. The Recipients can accept or reject the Allocator's decision. If they accept the decision, the money is divided according to the Allocator's split. If they reject the decision, both parties receive nothing. This is a one-time, take-it-or-leave-it decision, not a negotiation.

In a typical class, many of the Allocators opt for a 50-50 split, which is acceptable to the Recipients. But other Allocators become greedy, giving the Recipients, say, $100 and keeping $900 for themselves. In these cases the Recipients usually reject the split, so that both sides end up with nothing.

When I question the Recipients about their BATNA, they realize that it is zero. So if they were economically-rational individuals, they would accept one cent as their share of the split. But, instead, many of them insist on well over $100.

When I then ask the Recipients to explain why they decide to reject amounts well above their BATNA, the answers boil down to fairness. They do not think that it is fair for the Allocators to give them a small percentage of the total and are willing to give up hundreds of dollars to punish the Allocators.

There are two lessons from this exercise. First, because fair treatment is important to the other side in a negotiation, developing a reputation for fairness might reduce your transaction costs in future negotiations.

For example, when companies are sold, the parties typically spend millions of dollars during the negotiation process in due diligence. But when Warren Buffet decided to buy a $23 million company from Wal-Mart, the parties held a two-hour meeting that concluded with a handshake. Why? Wal-Mart had a solid reputation. In Buffet's words, "We did no 'due diligence.' We knew everything would be exactly as Wal-Mart said it would be—and it was." (Covey, *The Speed of Trust*)

The second lesson from the ultimatum exercise is to make sure you understand the role of fairness in your own decision making. Are you willing to make a large financial sacrifice to punish someone who has treated you unfairly? When someone cheats you illegally, are you prepared to spend the time and money necessary to pursue litigation? There is no harm in making decisions where your notions of fairness trump financial consid-erations—as long as you are aware of what is driving your behavior and the consequences.

Unethical Behavior by the Other Side

So far in this chapter we have focused on guidelines you can follow when faced with ethical dilemmas. But what if you think the other side is acting unethically? Can you tell when the other side is lying during a negotiation? There is good news and bad news.

The bad news is that it is very difficult to tell when someone is lying. Researchers have concluded that stereotypes about liars averting their gaze or clearing their throats are myths. (And there is no evidence that liars' noses are longer!) In one study, a researcher was able to identify only 31 human lie detectors out of 13,000 people who were tested. ("Deception Detection," *Science News*, July 27, 2004)

The good news is that negotiators are probably more willing to deceive the other side by omission (misleading the other side by saying nothing) than by making false representations. Researchers have identified an omission bias, the human tendency to think that immoral action is worse than immoral inaction. The lesson here is that when you question the other side rigorously they might be unwilling to tell a direct lie, thus enabling you to uncover their deceptive omissions.

Key takeaway. When faced with ethical dilemmas during negotia-tions, use the three law-based ethical standards for guidance: fraud, fiduciary duty and unconscionability. Before entering into

II USE KEY STRATEGIES AND TACTICS DURING NEGOTIATIONS

5 Develop Your Relationships and Power

Once you have finished your preparation by determining the type of negotiation, conducting a negotiation analysis, and deciding how to address ethical questions, you are now ready to dive into the negotiation. At the outset of the negotiation you should focus on two preliminary matters that are covered in this chapter: getting to know the other side on a personal level and developing your power.

BUILD RELATIONSHIPS BY GETTING TO KNOW THE OTHER SIDE ON A PERSONAL LEVEL

The old show tune "Getting to Know You" from *The King and I* should be the theme song for negotiators, as I discovered first-hand during an international negotiation. As Associate Dean at the University of Michigan's Ross School of Business I wanted to establish a center for our executive education programs in Europe following the success of a similar center in Hong Kong.

I learned that a new French university was under construction in Paris and I hoped the school would be willing to rent us space to run our programs. So I scheduled a half-day negotiation with the President of the new university and the Dean of its business school. I anticipated that this would be a difficult negotiation because real estate in Paris is so expensive.

I flew to Paris with two faculty members for the meeting. The evening before the negotiation, the President and Dean invited us to dinner at a quaint restaurant on the Left Bank (*Rive Gauche*). Over the course of a long relaxed dinner, we learned that the President had completed his doctoral dissertation on the English poet William Blake. As it turned out, one of the faculty members from Michigan was a William Blake fanatic and the two of them spent the evening rhapsodizing over the wonders of his poetry.

Fortunately, the negotiations the following morning took only thirty minutes instead of a half day and the university gave us a much better deal on the real estate than we anticipated. I owe this to William Blake and the rapport that we developed the evening before the negotiation. In short, they trusted us.

"Getting to Know You" is emphasized more in some cultures than others. For example, in China developing a relationship with someone you trust is considered more important than negotiating a lengthy legal contract. According to prominent businessman Sir Paul Judge, one reason for this is that "The courts in China are very slow when it comes to processes, so it is more important to know the person than it is probably in the West." ("Blending Confucius with Aristotle," *China Daily*, June 13, 2014)

In some western cultures, like the United States, negotiators often want to begin business negotiations immediately and don't want to take time to get to know the other side. Of course, this trait is not limited to US negotiators (and recall from the Chapter 2 discussion of cross-cultural negotiation that there are many variations within a culture).

For instance, a lawyer from Singapore in my executive course related a story about free trade negotiations. She was on a team of Singaporeans selected to negotiate a free trade agreement in India. The Singaporeans tried to move immediately to their agenda and didn't want to spend time getting to know their Indian counterparts. As a result, the negotiations failed. But after cross-cultural training back home by the former Ambassador from Singapore to India, they returned to India and were successful in reaching an agreement.

Getting to know the other side over a meal can have additional benefits. Research by Lakshmi Balachandra of Babson indicates that negotiators who eat together produce better results. Noting that "In Russia and Japan, important business dealings are conducted almost exclusively while dining and drinking and in the US many negotiations begin with 'Let's do lunch,'" she developed two experiments to determine whether dining while negotiating produced better outcomes. Her conclusion: Negotiators who combined eating and negotiating "created significantly increased profits compared to those who negotiated without dining." (http://blogs.hbr.org/2013/01/should-you-eat-while-you-negot/)

Getting to know the other side in a digital age brings special challenges. For one, some experts conclude that in our online world, conversation is becoming a lost art. The following quotes on developing conversational intelligence from a *Wall Street Journal* article, while not based on hard-core research, provide useful advice when you are attempting to converse with the other side prior to a negotiation.

- [B]e careful not to talk too much. This means you should avoid your favorite topic . . . .

- Ask a lot of questions. People love to talk about themselves and often will think you are a great conversationalist if you talk about them . . . .

- Listening is crucial. Dan Nainan, 32, a comedian from Manhattan, has learned to summarize what the other person says. ("So you think that . . ." or "So what you're saying is . . . .") "A conversation can go on indefinitely if you do this," he says.

("How to Be a Better Conversationalist," *Wall Street Journal*, Aug. 12, 2013)

Another challenge is that negotiations themselves are increasingly taking place online. As a result, it is more difficult to connect with the other side. This is unfortunate because brain-imaging research conducted by Dr. Srini Pillay of the Harvard Medical School shows that our mirror neuron activity during "face-to-face dialogue . . . creates brain synchrony that results in a feeling of connection." (*Entrepreneur*, August 2014) And studies by researchers at Harvard and the University of Chicago have concluded that handshakes at the beginning of negotiations promote cooperation between negotiators and reduce lying. (*Handshaking Promotes Cooperative Dealmaking*, Schroeder, et al.)

When face-to-face interaction is not possible there is an alternative approach. Negotiators who schmoozed on the phone with the other side for five minutes before conducting e-mail negotiations "were more than four times more likely to reach agreement" than negotiators who did not engage in this small talk, according to research conducted by Janice Nadler of Northwestern Law School. (*Negotiation*, March 2007)

Key takeaway. Before diving into a negotiation get to know the other side on a personal level. This strategy is important even when negotiations are online.

DEVELOP YOUR POWER

There are two sources of power in negotiation. First, information in general is an important source of power. Second, specific information about your and the other side's BATNA (best alternative to a negotiated agreement) can be used to increase your power and weaken the power of the other side.

Gather General Information from the Other Side

I have noticed that many business leaders and students begin my course thinking that their goal in negotiations is to persuade the other side to give them what they want. They soon learn that negotiation success depends more on asking questions to harvest information than on persuasion.

In the words of prominent Wharton professor Richard Shell in his book *Bargaining for Advantage*, "The research on negotiation effectiveness repeatedly underscores a simple fact about skilled negotiators: They focus more than average negotiators do on *receiving*, as opposed to delivering, information." Joel Kahn, my late colleague and teaching partner at the University of Michigan, put it more simply when he reminded his students that there is a reason God gave us two ears and only one mouth.

To "receive" information, negotiators must not only ask questions; they must listen carefully to answers. The ability to listen distinguishes skilled negotiators from average negotiators and it is also an important leadership skill. I worked for several years with a large international consulting firm. Over lunch one day I posed this question to one of the firm's leaders: "You have worked with business leaders around the world. Why is it that some very talented individuals end up in middle-management positions while others move on to leadership roles?"

Without hesitation he responded that those who move on to leadership roles possess two important attributes. First, they have a strong conceptual knowledge of their business. Second, they have the ability "to hear." By that he meant the ability to listen. There are signs that as organizations become flatter and leaner the ability to listen is becoming even more important. As legendary management expert Peter Drucker put it, "The leader of the past knew how to tell, the leader of the future will know how to ask." (Goldsmith, *Five Global Leadership Factors*)

ely, the results from brain-scanning studies indicate
f the world's population is biologically challenged in
the abin., to develop the listening skills that are so important in
negotiation and leadership. Specifically, males are able to listen
with only half their brains. Women probably realized this long
before the brain studies! ("Study Confirms What Women Know:
Men Listen Less," *Los Angeles Times*, November 29, 2000)

BATNA Power Strategies

As you question the other side during negotiations, one piece of
information is especially valuable—their BATNA. The ability to
walk away from a negotiation because there is a better alternative
provides you and the other side with a source of power. This
leads to three BATNA strategies.

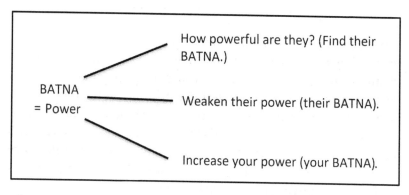

First, question the other side about their alternatives in an attempt
to find their BATNA and determine how powerful they are. But
remember that they may question you for the same reason. Will
you disclose your BATNA or attempt to hide it? The answer
usually depends on the strength of your best alternative. If it is
strong, you will probably be glad to disclose; if weak, you will
attempt to hide your BATNA.

For example, I live near Detroit, Michigan, a center for the automobile industry. If I work for a large manufacturer and you are

one of my suppliers with whom I am negotiating I will probably tell you my BATNA before I say "good morning" to you. For instance, I will tell you that if you don't agree to my terms I will go to one of the other suppliers who are lined up outside our meeting room.

Your second BATNA strategy is to attempt to weaken the other side's power by changing the perception of their BATNA. When I start talking about moving to another supplier you should emphasize the quality of your products, your record of on-time delivery, your history of willingness to work with my customers, our joint new product development efforts, and so on. After this discussion, moving to another supplier might not be as attractive as I thought.

Your third BATNA strategy is to increase your power by strengthening your BATNA. Do you rely too heavily on business with my automobile company? Can you increase your business with other companies? Can you develop new lines of business beyond the automobile industry? In the words of one senior executive, "You would never do a deal without talking to anyone else. Never." ("AOL's Rough Riders," *The Standard*, October 30, 2000)

Coalition bargaining. When several parties are involved in a negotiation, the power strategy can become more complex. For example, a friend of mine, let's call him Joe, was involved in negotiations with two other individuals—call them Cynthia and Sadie—over the formation of a business that would run a tennis center. Cynthia, let's assume, was a nationally-known, retired tennis player. Let's also assume that Sadie was well-known in the tennis community where the center would be based and Joe was a less-known local tennis instructor.

The three entrepreneurs planned to contribute an equal amount of capital and none of them would work for the tennis center. They anticipated that Cynthia's national fame would bring in half the revenue, Sadie's local fame would bring 30% of the revenue and the remaining 20% of the revenue would be derived from Joe's contacts. They needed, we will assume, at least two of the three partners to form the business.

In negotiations like this, BATNA calculations are difficult, if not impossible, because there are so many possible combinations. For example, Cynthia and Sadie could form a partnership that would bring in 80% of the total revenue, but Cynthia might become greedy and demand most of that amount. Sadie might be better off partnering with Joe and taking a large cut of their 50% of the revenue, but Cynthia then might offer Joe a better deal, and so on.

Given the instability that results from the many possible combinations, calculating a BATNA is unrealistic. So power might develop, instead, from a sense of trust between the parties or it might come from a reliance on principles. As the weakest party, for instance, Joe should emphasize the importance of fairness and equality among the partners, which might translate into equal division of income.

Key takeaway. Information is an important source of power in a negotiation, especially information about the other side's BATNA. Your BATNA strategy is to discover and weaken the other side's BATNA while improving your own BATNA.

6 Understand the Role of Agents in Negotiations

Often in negotiations, especially business negotiations, the other side will be represented by an agent. Because the use of agents is so common in the business world, you should have a basic understanding of agency relationships. In essence, agency creates an eternal triangle that involves a principal, an agent and a third party. For example, employees are agents who negotiate with third parties on behalf of a business (the principal).

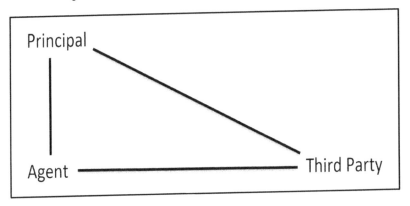

This chapter focuses primarily on negotiations through the eyes of a third party (you) who is negotiating with an agent acting on behalf of a principal. But before turning to this main theme, we first look at a different question. What factors should you, acting as a principal, use in deciding whether to use an agent in negotiations?

Use Five Factors in Deciding Whether to Use an Agent

Two of my former students have become sports agents. One represented University of Michigan graduate Chris Webber when he signed a contract with a National Basketball Association (NBA) team. The other former student, one of the most successful agents in the business, represents Kobe Bryant and 17 other NBA players.

Suppose that you are a college basketball star ready to begin your pro career. Should you negotiate through an agent, such as these former students? There are five key factors to consider—the same factors that are important when you decide whether to negotiate a business deal or the settlement of a lawsuit through an agent.

Who is the better negotiator—you or the agent? In answering this question you should do a cost-benefit analysis by comparing the benefits of using a negotiator who has better skills than you with the compensation that the agent will receive.

Does the agent have experience with the issues that will arise in your negotiation? If you are negotiating an NBA contract, you probably don't want a real estate agent to represent you.

Does the negotiation involve a technical matter that requires special expertise? If you are negotiating with a licensee who is interested in using your technology, you probably will hire someone with expertise in intellectual property. If the negotiation involves complex legal issues, you should probably negotiate through an attorney.

How much time do you have for the negotiation and what are the opportunity costs? If you own or manage a business, your time might be better spent developing products and services for your customers.

What is your relationship with the other side? If you are negotiating the resolution of a dispute, it often makes sense to bring in agents who have no personal involvement and can distance themselves from the dispute.

Clarify Authority When Negotiating with Agents

When you are a third party negotiating with an agent, there is one key issue you should address at the beginning of the negotiation: Does the agent have authority to do a deal on behalf of the principal? If the answer is no, then the negotiation is often a waste of time. This question is complicated by the fact that there are three types of authority that the agent might possess: express authority, implied authority, and apparent authority.

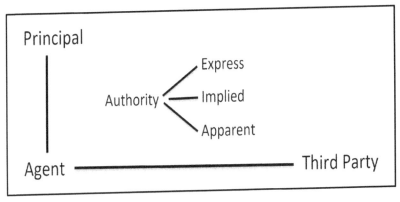

Express authority. Express authority is easy to analyze. Did the principal expressly authorize the agent to negotiate the contract? If so, the agent has authority. For example, companies commonly give certain employee-agents authority to use company checking accounts. If an agent (say, a company accountant) embezzles company funds by writing checks to himself, the company (and not the bank) bears the loss because of the express authority given to the agent.

Implied authority. The second type of authority, implied authority, is a bit more complicated. Even when not expressly stated by the principal, agents have implied authority to perform the normal duties associated with their position. For example, a manager hired by a business has implied authority to purchase equipment, hire and fire employees, pay company debts, and so on.

Apparent authority. The third type of authority, apparent authority, is even more complex. Apparent authority arises in situations where, although the agent has no real authority, the principal's actions mislead the third party into thinking that authority exists.

For example, let's assume that you own a business that has contracted for several years with a group of suppliers. You sell the business, its trade name and the list of suppliers to a buyer. The buyer immediately orders supplies from one of the suppliers, but doesn't make payment. Are you liable? You didn't give express authority to the buyer and there is no evidence of implied authority because you didn't hire the buyer. However, there is apparent authority based on your past dealings with suppliers. You should have notified them when you sold the business.

Apparent authority can complicate your negotiation strategy. Assume that you hire an agent to purchase equipment from a manufacturer. You give the agent a letter of authority, which she presents to the manufacturer. Privately, you give your agent a reservation price—for example, you tell the agent not to pay more than $90,000 for the equipment. If the agent then buys the equipment for $100,000 are you liable on the contract? Yes, because the agent had apparent authority that arose from the letter of authority. This authority exists even though the agent had no actual authority to make the purchase for over $90,000.

Decide whether authority exists. Given the importance of deciding whether your counterpart in a negotiation has authority, how do you determine whether authority exists? To illustrate the answer to this important question, suppose that you work as a loan officer at a bank. Brett is negotiating with you to borrow $25,000 for personal purposes.

Bank policy requires Brett to provide security in case the loan is not repaid. Brett works for a successful company, and the general manager of the company is willing to sign a loan guarantee on behalf of the company. The guarantee states that "This guaranty is signed by an officer having legal right to bind the company thru authorization of the Board of Directors."

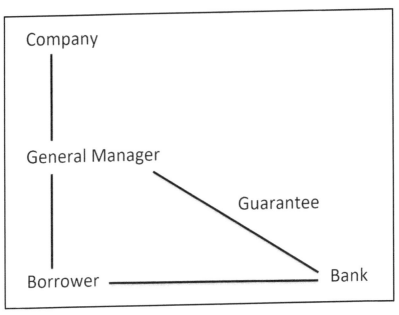

Assuming that you are familiar with Brett's company and know that it is financially sound, would you make the loan? In a Michigan case, *In re Union City Milk Co.* (46 N.W.2d 361), a bank that made the loan learned a painful lesson. When the borrower did not repay the loan, the bank sued the company on the basis of the guarantee.

The court decided that the company was not liable. The company had given no express authority to the manager to guarantee the employee's personal loan and there was no implied authority because the ability to guarantee personal loans is not within the normal responsibilities of a manager. The loss fell on the bank.

Where did the loan officer (who is now probably unemployed) go astray? The loan officer did a good job in obtaining a guarantee in writing and the guarantee stated that the manager had authority to make the guarantee. The problem is that the wrong person—the agent—made the statement that he had authority. The important message here: When you are negotiating a deal, never ask an agent whether he has authority. Instead, always address this question to the principal (in this case, the company's Board of Directors).

Secret agents. Occasionally you will negotiate with an agent without realizing it. Businesses use secret agents for a variety of reasons and, although there might be exceptions under local law, you are bound by the contracts you negotiate with them.

For example, Walt Disney built Disneyland in Los Angeles on a relatively small parcel of real estate that soon became landlocked by surrounding businesses. When Disney later planned Disney World in Florida, he decided to acquire a much larger property. But he realized that if owners knew he was buying their property, prices would skyrocket.

To keep prices low he hired secret agents to acquire the property. Eventually he amassed over 27,000 acres, "about twice the size of Manhattan, the same size as San Francisco . . . . Once word got out that it was Disney, prices jumped from $183 per acre to around $1,000 per acre overnight. But by then, Walt had purchased all his land . . . ." (http://www.mouseplanet.com/)

To complicate matters, occasionally the person with whom you are negotiating plays a double role as both agent and principal. A friend of mine is a great negotiator and has been very successful in business. He told me a story about negotiations that involved his purchase of a company from the owner. They met at the owner's beautiful home in the Black Forest in Germany. My friend had done lots of research on the company in preparation for the negotiations. He and the owner reviewed the terms of the deal while eating delicious pastries served by a housekeeper.

Finally my friend asked the owner whether the terms were okay. He then noticed the owner looking out of the corner of his eye at the housekeeper in the background, who shook her head "no." My friend suddenly realized that she had authority that he had overlooked when preparing for negotiations.

He later learned that the housekeeper was the long-term mistress of the owner and that she was going to receive a large percentage of the sales price! So the owner was negotiating on her behalf as well as his own. The good news is that eventually my friend acquired the company—and in the process learned a useful lesson about searching for hidden principals!

Key takeaway. Ask five key questions when deciding whether to use an agent during negotiations. At the beginning of negotiations find out whether the agent has authority to make a deal by asking the principal (rather than the agent).

7 Use Psychological Tools—and Avoid Psychological Traps

This chapter covers psychological tools that you can use in negotiation, which are also traps that you want to avoid when used by the other side. These tools are especially important because they are useful in financial and leadership decision making beyond negotiation. This chapter serves as a checklist to keep handy for use when making all types of decisions.

The chapter cites several books that are recommended if you want to pursue this topic further. The best of these books, one that I highly recommend, is *Judgment in Managerial Decision Making* by Bazerman and Moore. Other recommended books cited in this chapter are:

- *Decision Traps* by Russo and Schoemaker

- *Influence: The Psychology of Persuasion* by Cialdini

- *Negotiating Rationally* by Bazerman and Neale

As Bazerman and Moore point out, there are two basic types of research on decision making. One type—prescriptive decision making—focuses on how we should make decisions. An example is decision tree analysis, which was discussed in Chapter 3. With this approach, you can clarify your decision making by drawing a picture of the decision in tree form, assigning probabilities, and calculating an expected value.

The other type of research on decision making—descriptive decision making—focuses on how humans actually make decisions. As noted by Bazerman and Moore, in making decisions we rely on simple rules of thumb called heuristics. Here is an example, similar to one in their book. Suppose that your company needs a financial analyst. You have decided to recruit only at the top ten MBA programs. That is your heuristic.

How can you criticize this heuristic? Without this heuristic, you might find that the best candidate for your job opening is not at one of the top ten schools. For a variety of financial and personal reasons, many talented individuals do not attend leading schools. And you might be able to hire this person at a lower salary than what a student at a leading school would demand. How can you defend this heuristic? Over time, you are likely to find better candidates at the better schools. And by limiting the number of schools, you reduce your travel and other search costs.

The cost-benefit analysis used in developing a heuristic like this can help you navigate through a complex, uncertain world. The good news, as Bazerman and Moore point out, is that heuristics are useful. However, because heuristics can also lead to serious error, understanding them is important for negotiators and other decision makers.

We now turn to nine tools or guidelines you can use in future negotiations. They are based on descriptive decision making research, some of which focuses on biases related to our use of heuristics.

1. Don't Assume a Fixed Pie

We live in a competitive world characterized by sporting events. Someone wins the Masters golf tournament; others lose. Someone wins the Wimbledon tennis tournament; others lose. One team wins the World Cup; other teams lose.

We bring this sense of competition into negotiations by assuming that they are competitions for slices in a fixed pie in which one side wins and the other side loses. As Bazerman and Moore note, the fixed pie assumption is a fundamental bias that distorts negotiators' behavior: "When negotiating over an issue, they assume that their interests necessarily and *directly* conflict with the other party's interests."

After recognizing this bias, your challenge is to ask whether the other side's interests are really in conflict with your own. By conducting an interests analysis that lists your and the other side's interests side by side, you might be able to find interests that are not in conflict. For example, Chapter 2 discussed a simple negotiation over a gourmet anchovy pizza. Each side wanted the pizza. That was their position. The pizza was the mythical—and literal—fixed pie.

However, what were each side's interests and were these interests "directly in conflict"? When asked why they wanted the pizza, they discovered that one side's interest was the crust and the other side's interest was the center of the pizza—everything but the crust. By recognizing that the fixed pie assumption was a myth in this negotiation, they were able to develop a solution that satisfied their interests.

Reactive devaluation. A special challenge in overcoming the mythical fixed pie assumption is something that researchers call "reactive devaluation." That is, when the other side in a negotiation makes a proposal, we react to it by devaluing it without considering the merits simply because it comes from the other side.

In one study by Stillinger and others, for example, the researchers gave an arms reduction proposal to individuals in the United States and told them that it came from President Reagan. Ninety percent thought that it was neutral or favored the United States. When the researchers gave the same proposal to other individuals and told them it came from President Gorbachev of Russia, this dropped to 44%. For a summary of reactive devaluation research, see http://en.wikipedia.org/wiki/Reactive_devaluation, where other studies are cited.

I see the impact of reactive devaluation in my courses. I give students an exercise that involves litigation between their employer, a company that sells a software package, and its licensee. When the licensee proposes a reasonable settlement, most students reject the offer because they think that it must indicate that the licensee has a weak case. By focusing on the source of the proposal, the licensee, rather than on the substance of the offer, they miss an opportunity to negotiate an agreement that would avoid considerable litigation expense.

2. Consider Anchoring When Developing a First-Offer Strategy

As noted by Bazerman and Neale and other researchers, humans tend to anchor on an initial value when estimating the value of uncertain objects. For example, try this experiment developed by Russo and Schoemaker. Add 400 to the last three digits of your phone number and write down the total.

Now consider this: Attila the Hun was one of the feared conquerors in world history. He was eventually defeated during the Common Era (that is, A.D.). Was he defeated before or after the number that you wrote down? After writing down "before" or "after," write down the year in which you think that Attila the Hun was defeated.

When I run this experiment in class, the results are often similar to the following:

Last 3 digits of phone number + 400	Date of defeat of Attila the Hun
400–599	580
600–799	670
800–999	920
1000–1199	1210
1200–1399	1340

If you are a scientist looking at these results, what might you conclude? It appears that the numbers selected for the date of defeat on the right are influenced by the numbers on the left. That is, as the numbers on the left increase, so do the numbers on the right.

What is the relationship between the phone numbers and Attila the Hun? There is no relationship. Because my students are uncertain about the date of defeat, they anchor on the only number available—the last three digits of their phone numbers plus 400. (Incidentally, Attila the Hun was defeated in 451 A.D.)

Anchoring has a powerful effect even on experts in a particular area. For example, researchers gave a group of physicians a case describing a patient who might have lung disease. The physicians were asked to state whether the chances of this person having the disease were higher or lower than 1%. They were then asked to estimate the chances that the patient had lung disease.

The researchers then gave another group of physicians the same case and asked them whether the chances of the patient having lung disease were higher or lower than 90%. These doctors then guessed the chances that the person had lung disease.

The first group of physicians anchored on the low, random probability they were given (1%); the second group anchored on the high, random probability they were given (90%). As a result, when they estimated the chances that the patient had lung disease, the second group's estimate was 29% higher on average than that of the first group. (Brewer, et al., *The Influence of Irrelevant Anchors on the Judgments and Choices of Doctors and Patients*)

First-offer strategy. How does anchoring affect negotiation? An important question that arises during negotiations is: Who should make the first offer? I've asked business executives around the world this question and the result is usually the same: Always let the other side make the first offer.

They often back this up with examples from their own experience. A retired executive, for instance, recently told me about a real estate negotiation in which he expected to pay around $300,000 for a lot, but paid considerably less after the other side opened with a price of $35,000.

As an aside, when the other side makes an unexpectedly favorable opening offer, do not accept it immediately unless you want to make your counterpart feel bad. A friend recounted the story of a senior executive at his company who had a conflict with a new CEO. The new CEO wanted to get rid of him and asked: "What will it take for you to retire?" The senior executive gave him a highly inflated number, which the CEO immediately accepted. This caused the executive to experience regret as he wondered whether his inflated number was too low!

How does the conventional wisdom—always let the other side propose the first number—relate to anchoring theory? Anchoring would suggest that you should propose the first number so that you can anchor the other side to your number.

Which side is correct—the experienced executives who advocate the conventional wisdom (let the other side make the first offer) or the anchoring proponents? The answer is complicated and difficult to generalize. For example, research by my University of Michigan colleague Shirli Kopelman and others indicates that negotiators who make the first offer do better economically but are less satisfied with outcomes because they feel more anxiety. ("Resolving the First-Offer Dilemma," *Negotiation*, July 2007)

Given the complexity of the question, here is a recommended rule of thumb. Follow the conventional wisdom when the value of the item sold is uncertain. By asking the other side to propose the first number, you gather information about the item's value. (Of course, in so doing try to avoid being trapped by the other side's anchor.) On the other hand, if you are quite certain about the value of the item, you should ignore the conventional wisdom and try to anchor the other side to your number.

What if you are in a stalemate because you decide to ask the other side to propose the first number but they want your number first? You might try an information exchange. Lawyers use this approach in lawsuit settlement negotiations. For example, social scientist Herbert Kritzer has noted a pattern where "discussions concerning damages may be less a series of offers and counteroffers and more a process of exchange of information." (*Let's Make a Deal*)

3. Avoid Overconfidence

As noted by Bazerman and Moore, overconfidence, like anchoring, is the result of our use of heuristics. Essentially, we are overconfident that our decisions are correct. Try the following test to determine whether you are overconfident. For each of the following, write down a range so that you are 90% confident that your answer is correct. Do not look at the answers that follow and do not look for answers online. To succeed you should answer 9 of the 10 questions correctly. Why not 100%? This would be too easy because you could select broad ranges for each item.

1.   Year in which Wolfgang Amadeus Mozart was born

    _____ _____

2.   Length of the Nile River

    _____ _____

3.   Number of times lightning strikes the earth per minute

    _____ _____

4.   Time it takes sunlight to reach the earth

    _____ _____

5.   Diameter of the moon

    _____ _____

6.   Number of knives, forks and spoons in the White House

    _____ _____

7.   Number of actively spoken languages in the world

    _____ _____

8.   Gestation period (in days) of an Asian elephant

    _____ _____

9.   Number of pregnancies that take place daily worldwide

    _____ _____

10.   Length of time (in days) a snail can sleep if it isn't disturbed

    _____ _____

Here are the answers:

1.   Mozart was born in 1756.

2.   The Nile River is 4,187 miles long.

3.   Lightning strikes the earth 6,000 times per minute.

4. It takes sunlight 492 seconds to reach the earth.

5. The diameter of the moon is 2,160 miles.

6. There are 13,092 knives, forks and spoons in the White House.

7. There are an estimated 6,000 actively-spoken languages in the world.

8. The gestation period of an Asian elephant is 645 days.

9. There are an estimated 365,000 conceptions daily.

10. A snail can sleep 1,095 days if not disturbed.

(From Russo and Schoemaker, *Statistic Brain, and Odd Trivia Facts* (Rich Hancock))

Were you successful in meeting the challenge? Did you answer 9 out of the 10 questions correctly? If you were not successful, there is bad news and good news. The bad news is that, like most people, you were overconfident in selecting ranges that were too narrow. The good news is that virtually the only people who aren't overconfident on a regular basis are clinically depressed! ("Saving Yourself from Yourself," *Business Week*, October 10, 1999)

Overconfidence is a trap that business school professors love to study. For example, finance professors have concluded that overconfidence in making investment decisions can lead to losses. Accounting professors have observed overconfidence when managers predict long-term earnings.

Overconfidence can also affect your negotiating strategy. I have noticed that in preparing for negotiation, students tend to predict ZOPAs (zones of potential agreement) that are too narrow. This impacts their evaluation of the facts and their negotiation strategy. One consequence is that it can cause them to become too modest in establishing stretch goals.

Decision making vs. decision implementation. Occasionally, senior executives will challenge me when I discuss overconfidence. They claim that overconfidence is a good trait because it enables them, as business leaders, to encourage their employees to do more than they ever thought possible.

Overconfidence has also been touted as something good for entrepreneurs because it "may provide the vision necessary to convince potential hires and investors of the opportunity to get in on the ground floor of a growing startup. Optimism may also lead founders to see the best in people and thus contribute to their social skills." (Wasserman, *Cognitive Biases in Founder Decision Making*)

I agree with these sentiments to some extent. When you *implement* decisions, a good dose of optimism is healthy. However, when you make decisions you should be a *realist* and search for disconfirming evidence to improve your decision making process.

Using disconfirming evidence can be a challenge. I give my students a sequence of numbers, 2-4-6, and ask them to guess the rule that I used in developing this sequence. (The rule is that the numbers increase in value.) Before they give me their answer, I give them a chance to test their guesses by giving me three additional numbers. They invariably give me numbers that match their guesses instead of providing disconfirming evidence.

For example, suppose that a student thinks that my rule is "increase the previous number by 2." As a test, the student would give me evidence that confirms the guess, 8-10-12. If the student had used disconfirming evidence, say, 8-9-10, I would tell her that this guess meets my rule (increasing numbers) and she would immediately realize that her rule (numbers increase by 2) was incorrect.

The key lesson is to try to avoid this "confirming evidence trap" by seeking disconfirming evidence when making decisions. (This experiment is described in Bazerman and Chugh, "Decisions Without Blinders," *Harvard Business Review*. See also Hammond et al., "The Hidden Traps in Decision Making," *Harvard Business Review*.)

One way that business leaders can avoid the trap is to encourage constructive conflict when decisions are made. For example, a prominent Delaware judge has recommended that boards of directors should appoint a devil's advocate to ensure that the board does not become too deferential when considering a CEO's proposals. ("Cognitive Bias in Director Decision-Making," *Corporate Governance Advisor*, November/December 2012)

4. Frame Choices to Your Advantage

The way that we frame questions can have a huge impact on decisions. For example, suppose that you are the Director of Public Health in a city that is preparing for an unusual strain of flu virus that you anticipate will kill 600 senior citizens. Your two top assistants, Thelma and Louise, have developed plans for combatting the disease. With Thelma's plan, 200 of the 600 seniors will be saved. With Louise's plan, there is a 1/3 chance that all 600 seniors will be saved and 2/3 chance that none of them will survive. Thelma and Louise have been negotiating unsuccessfully over which plan to adopt and they now want you to decide. Which plan would you select?

Now assume that you ask Thelma and Louise to go back to the drawing board to develop alternative plans. Thelma comes up with a plan where 400 of the senior citizens will die. Under Louise's plan, there is a 1/3 chance that no one will die and a 2/3 chance that 600 seniors will die. Here again, they are unsuccessful in negotiating an agreement and they ask you to decide.

Which plan would you select?

This scenario is based on research by Amos Tversky and Daniel Kahneman ("The Framing of Decisions and the Psychology of Choice," *Science*) and is also discussed in Bazerman and Neale. Tversky and Kahneman discovered that in the first situation, almost three-fourths of participants in their study selected Thelma's plan, while in the second situation, close to 80% selected Louise's plan. These results are striking because the plans in the two situations are identical. For example, in both of Thelma's plans 400 senior citizens will die.

What caused the difference in results? In the first situation your choice is framed in terms of saving people, which is a gain—a positive choice. In the second situation your choice is framed in terms of senior citizens dying, which is a loss—a negative choice. When faced with gains people become risk averse and select the sure thing (Thelma's plan that saves 200 senior citizens). When faced with losses people are more willing to take chances (Louise's plan where there is a 1/3 chance that no one will die and a 2/3 chance that 600 seniors will die).

This is a powerful tool in negotiations with your boss, members of your team, your customers, or negotiators from other companies. Framing the choices you give them as either gains or losses has a significant impact on their decisions.

5. Look Beyond Easily-Available Information

What causes more death annually in the United States—car accidents or lung cancer? When I ask this question in class, a large percentage of the students select car accidents. Even when I ask this question when teaching negotiation in a major medical center, a high percentage of the doctors in the seminar select the same answer.

These results are surprising because in a typical year around four times as many Americans die from lung cancer than in car accidents. So what accounts for these erroneous conclusions? Our decisions are overly influenced by information that is easily available. As noted by Russo and Schoemaker in discussing the lung cancer example, "People seem to implicitly assume that the information that is most easily available to them is also the most relevant information." Information about car accidents is easily available through news reports that are sometimes accompanied by gruesome pictures. Death from lung cancer is not front page news and often is not even mentioned in an obituary.

Understanding the availability trap can be useful during negotiations. For example, I once worked with an executive from an aircraft manufacturer. Hundreds of millions of dollars were at stake when the company negotiated contracts with the government, and government officials often delayed their decisions for months following the negotiations. The executive told me that the manufacturer produced videos, which showed its fighter planes in action during bombing operations, for use during negotiations. The company hoped that these videos, like pictures of car accidents, would easily come to mind when government officials awarded contracts.

6. Beware of Dollar Auction Traps

In my course I occasionally auction off a $20 bill. The rules of the auction are simple. Bids are made in increments of $1. The high bidder gets the $20, but the second highest bidder also pays me and receives nothing. So if Sara is the highest bidder with a bid of $14, she wins $20, while if Pete is second highest at $12, he pays me and receives nothing in return. Typically, several students in class begin bidding at the outset but as the bidding approaches $20 all but two drop out. These two often continue bidding well beyond $20.

Academics have derived a number of lessons from this devious game, which was invented by Professor Shubik of Yale. Three of these lessons are especially important in negotiation and dispute resolution.

Escalation of commitment. First, it is easy to fall into a trap where the parties irrationally escalate commitment, as in the dollar auction. Litigation provides an example. It is not unusual to hear about situations where one or both parties to the litigation each spend more than the amount in dispute. Like the two final bidders in a dollar auction, once they lock into litigation their costs escalate beyond rationality. The book by Bazerman and Moore includes an excellent chapter on escalation of commitment.

Competitive arousal. The second lesson is that a dollar auction can trigger what researchers call competitive arousal. According to an article in the *Harvard Business Review* (Malhotra, et al., "When Winning is Everything") this can arise when there is intense rivalry between two individuals who are in the spotlight (for instance, in a negotiation).

The dollar auction provides a perfect setting for competitive arousal. In one $20 auction conducted in an MBA class by a leading negotiation professor, Keith Murnighan, the winning bid was $15,000 and the losing bid was $14,500. And the rules required the bidders to pay! The winner realized that the amounts paid were going to charity and this was her way of making a charitable contribution. The losing bidder apparently became trapped by competitive arousal. He simply wanted to win.

As noted in the Malhotra article, you should try to minimize competitive arousal by reducing the intensity of the rivalry. In a negotiation, for instance, you might negotiate through an agent or use a team to handle the negotiations so that one person is not in the spotlight.

Other side's perspective. The third lesson from the dollar auction is the importance of looking at any negotiation from the perspective of the other side. At the beginning, the dollar auction looks great from your perspective in that you have a chance to win $20 with, say, a bid of $14. But when you consider the fact that there are forty or so other potential bidders in class with the same thoughts, the auction loses its attractiveness. This is an important lesson for all negotiations. As Bazerman and Neale put it: "We've found that managers who take into account the other side's perspective are most successful in negotiation simulations. This focus allows them to predict the other side's behavior."

I once had dinner with a senior executive who had been involved in financial negotiations with leading negotiators from around the world. When I asked him what distinguished a good negotiator from a great one, he didn't hesitate one second in responding: "The ability to look at the financials from the other side."

Here are a couple of challenges to test your ability to look at negotiations from the other side. The first challenge is based on a story in a great book called *The Manager as Negotiator* by Lax and Sebenius. Near the end of his campaign for the presidency, Teddy Roosevelt planned to use pamphlets with a picture of him looking very presidential. Just before his campaign team was ready to begin distributing the pamphlets they discovered that a photographer held the copyright to the picture.

Roosevelt's campaign did not have enough funds to pay for copyright permission and they did not want to use the picture illegally. Yet they felt that they needed the pamphlets to win the election. Unsure what to do, they asked a successful negotiator and Roosevelt supporter for advice. What would you do if they had asked for your advice?

This is what the Roosevelt supporter did. Apparently able to look at the negotiation from the other side, he sent a cable to the photographer that read (as quoted from *The Manager as Negotiator*): "We are planning to distribute many pamphlets with

Roosevelt's picture on the cover. It will be great publicity for the studio whose photograph we use. How much will you pay us to use yours? Respond immediately."

The response? The photographer offered to pay $250 if they used the photograph. This great negotiator had turned the table on the other side!

Here is another, more sophisticated (and mind-bending!) example from the Bazerman and Neale book. You work for a company that is considering an offer to buy another company ("Target"). The value of Target under current management is somewhere between $0 and $100 million, depending on the success of its oil drilling operations. Each value between $0 and $100 million is equally likely.

Target's owners know the exact value of the company because they have received reports about the success of the oil drilling operations. Under your management, Target's value will be 50% higher than the current value, whatever that is. How much would you bid for Target, assuming only one offer on a take-it-or-leave-it basis?

When I use this example in executive seminars, even finance experts cannot answer the question correctly. Why? They do not look at this deal from Target's perspective. Let's pick a random offer, say, $60 million. If the true value of the company is higher than $60 million, Target (which knows the true value of the company) will not accept the offer.

Stated another way, Target will only accept offers in the range of S0-$60 million, which have an average value of $30 million. Even after the 50% increase in value after your acquisition, the value becomes only $45 million, which is still less than your $60 million offer. Because the value will always be lower than any number that you bid, the correct answer is that you should bid $0.

The importance of looking at negotiations from the perspective of the other side is, of course, not limited to business deals. A friend of mine was a senior advisor to a US President. When briefing the President on, say, an upcoming meeting with a leader from another country, my friend would explain the key issues that affected the relationship between the two countries. He then observed the President's uncanny ability to discuss the issues from the perspective of the other side and to reframe the issues to address the other side's concerns.

7. Encourage Reciprocity

In his book *Influence*, Robert Cialdini devotes an entire chapter to "Reciprocation," the fundamental need that we, as humans, feel to repay someone who has done something for us. He quotes anthropologist Richard Leakey, who notes that reciprocity makes us human: "We are human because our ancestors learned to share their food and their skills in an honored network of obligation."

We can all think of examples of reciprocity. Let me share one that involved my negotiation with a young girl. One of my students invited me to participate in his wedding in Mumbai, India. One afternoon I had some free time and decided to go for a walk in the beautiful terraced gardens known as the Hanging Gardens at the top of Malabar Hill.

As I approached the gardens, a young street girl, probably eleven or twelve years old, approached me and wanted to sell me a fan made out of peacock feathers. After I told her I wasn't interested she followed me into the gardens and explained the topiary, vegetation, and structures in the gardens. What did I buy at the end of the tour? A peacock feather fan. The girl may have been young, but she had an intuitive understanding of the power of reciprocity.

Often overlooked in discussions of reciprocity is what has been called the "Ben Franklin effect," or what I call reverse reciprocity. Instead of doing something for someone else in the hopes that they will reciprocate, ask them to do something for you.

As Franklin put it, "He that has once done you a kindness will be more ready to do you another, than he whom you yourself have obliged." For example, in trying to secure the friendship of a rival, Franklin asked to borrow one of the rival's rare books. The rival obliged and in returning the book, Franklin thanked him profusely. They became good friends after that.

8. Use the Contrast Principle

When I purchased my first house, a real estate agent showed me the ugliest house I have ever seen. It needed considerable repairs and had a huge price. I told the agent that I wasn't interested. She then took me to a house that was attractive, but also needed lots of repairs and had a huge price. Again, I told her I wasn't interested. Then she took me to an attractive house that was well-maintained—and it too had a huge price. I immediately said "I'll take it."

What had she done to me psychologically? In real estate language, she had first taken me to "set-up" properties. In the language of psychology, she had trapped me by using the contrast principle. She realized that the third house would look quite different when shown in contrast to the first two than it would look in isolation. Had she taken me only to the third house I would not have been interested because of the high price.

The contrast principle is well known to retailers. For example, an executive in my negotiation seminar managed a high-end store in Singapore that sold purses for upwards of a thousand dollars. She directed her employees to place men's neckties next to the purses. Sales of the neckties were brisk because, although the ties were expensive, they looked cheap in comparison to the purse prices.

I have fallen into a similar trap. When buying a suit I often buy a tie that costs more than I would pay if buying it as a separate item. In contrast to the price of the suit, the tie seems to be reasonably priced.

The contrast principle is vividly illustrated by the following letter from a college student to her parents. There are many versions of this letter. One version is quoted in the Cialdini book; this one is from: www.netjeff.com/humor/item.cgi?file=DearMomAndDad.

> Dear Mom and Dad,
>
> It has now been three months since I left for college. I am sorry for my thoughtlessness in not having written before. I will bring you up to date but before you read on you had better sit down. Okay?
>
> I am getting along pretty well now. The skull fracture and concussion I got when I jumped out of my apartment window when it caught fire after my arrival here is pretty well healed. I only spent two weeks in the hospital and now I can see almost normally and only get these sick headaches once a day. Fortunately the fire and my jump were witnessed by Roger an attendant at the gas station, and he was the one who called the fire department. He also visited me in the hospital, and since I had nowhere to live he was kind enough to invite me to share his apartment with him. He is a very fine man, and we are planning to get married. We haven't set the date yet, but it will be before my pregnancy begins to show. His divorce is final now, and he shares custody of his 3 children.
>
> The reason for the delay in our marriage is that Roger has a minor infection which prevents us from passing our premarital blood tests, and I carelessly caught it from him. This will soon clear up with the penicillin injections I am taking daily.

Now that I have brought you up to date I want to tell you that there was no fire, I did not have a concussion or skull fracture, I was not in the hospital, I am not pregnant, I am not engaged, I do not have syphilis, and there is no divorced man in my life. However, I am getting a "D" in Art and an "F" in Biology and I wanted you to see these marks in the proper perspective.

Your loving daughter,

Jane

While Jane is having difficulties with Art and Biology, she should do very well in future negotiations because she clearly understands the contrast principle!

9. Take a Big-Picture Perspective

This last tool—or trap—is sometimes overlooked in books on negotiation: In a negotiation it is important to keep in mind the big picture even when you are immersed in the details. This is more difficult than it sounds because of what Bazerman and Chugh call "bounded awareness." ("Decisions Without Blinders," *Harvard Business Review*). An important aspect of bounded awareness is that our focus on one aspect of negotiation—say, price—might limit awareness of more important concerns.

An example of bounded awareness is the Monkey Business Illusion: http://www.youtube.com/watch?v=IGQmdoK_ZfY. In this video, members of two teams of basketball players, one wearing white shirts and the other wearing black shirts, pass a basketball to fellow team members. You are asked to count the number of passes made by the team wearing white shirts. While you are focused on this task, someone dressed as a gorilla walks to the middle of the two teams, pounds his chest and walks away. A large percentage of viewers completely miss the gorilla because they are so focused on counting the passes.

The Grand Bazaar in Istanbul is considered by some to be a shopper's paradise. With thousands of shops that line over sixty covered streets, the Grand Bazaar offers a chance to test your ability to negotiate by haggling over jewelry, furniture, carpets, clothes, leather goods and many touristy items. When I visited the bazaar I was told that many buyers become so enthralled by their negotiations within the Grand Bazaar that they overlook the big picture (or Big Gorilla), which is that goods are cheaper outside the Grand Bazaar where the local citizens shop.

There is considerable wisdom in the observations of veteran negotiator Marie-Christine Brochu of the International Air Transport Association: "When you negotiate, you need to always keep in mind the big picture . . . and always come back to it, to avoid the trap of being lost in the details." ("A Canadian Perspective on Contract Negotiation," *ACC Docket*, October, 2012)

Key takeaway. This chapter has provided a checklist of nine tools that you can use or traps you want to avoid in future negotiations. Keep this checklist handy for use when making decisions during negotiations and when making other leadership or financial decisions.

III CLOSE YOUR NEGOTIATION WITH A BINDING CONTRACT

8. Use Contract Law to Complete
Your Negotiation
9. Move Beyond Legalities to
Create Value

8   Use Contract Law to Complete Your Negotiation

It is often stated that negotiation takes place in the shadow of the law. The law actually casts two shadows on negotiations. First, in a negotiation to resolve a dispute, the shadow is litigation—the ultimate BATNA in this type of negotiation. Chapter 3 explored how the litigation BATNA in the US differs from that in other countries. That chapter also explained how to calculate the value of your litigation BATNA using decision tree analysis.

The second shadow, which arises in deal-making negotiations, is the legal framework for contract negotiation and the elements necessary to convert your agreement into a binding contract. Although the focus of this chapter is on these elements, we first step back from legal details to discuss three broad perspectives on contract law and two key variables that determine the law that will apply to your contract.

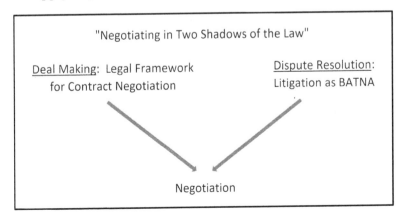

PERSPECTIVES ON CONTRACT LAW

In essence, a contract is an agreement enforceable by law. We all enter into many agreements that are not legally enforceable. For example, you and I can strongly agree that a certain movie is the worst one we have ever seen but our agreement is not enforceable in court. Contract law provides a framework for determining which of our agreements are enforceable.

Three perspectives are useful when thinking about contract law. First, there is a global perspective. In the global world of business, the rule of law is critically important when making business decisions. No legal rules are more important than contract law because contracts establish your rights and duties in business deals. Your first question when making investments in any country should be: Will my contract rights be respected and enforced in this country?

Second, from a company perspective, contracts are the key to business success. All other company activities—accounting, marketing, finance, strategy, etc.—are for naught if your contracts are not profitable. Within companies, value is created during contract negotiations and companies fail when these negotiations do not produce successful results.

Third, from a personal perspective, contracts (both written and unwritten) permeate our daily lives. Whether these contracts involve the simple purchase of a meal or more complex transactions such as buying a house, they represent an important aspect of our interactions with other humans.

Because contracts are so common in our business and personal lives, in most cases we must act as our own lawyers when negotiating them. In other words, we cannot have a lawyer at our elbow throughout the day to advise us whenever we enter into a business or personal contract. As a result, we need a fundamental understanding of the sources of contract law and the four key elements that determine whether a contract has been formed. We now turn to these topics.

UNDERSTAND THE SOURCES OF CONTRACT LAW

When you are involved in a negotiation and a contract law question arises, where can you (or an attorney) find the answer? Two key questions determine the source of contract law. First, are we in civil law or common law country? Second, what type of contract are we negotiating?

Type of Legal System

Although contract law in a globalized economy has become increasingly similar from country to country, differences still exist. The industrialized world is split between countries that have a civil law system and those with a common law system. At the beginning of any negotiation, you should determine which system governs your contract.

Generally speaking, civil law countries include Continental European countries and the former colonies of these countries. In civil law countries, the principles of law are primarily found in a "code"—in effect, an encyclopedia of law. In contrast, common law countries (generally England and its former colonies) rely more heavily on previously decided cases—that is, "precedents"—as a source of law.

The distinction between civil law and common law countries is especially important because the legal requirements for a valid contract differ to some extent between systems. For example, civil law does not include the consideration requirement discussed below.

Apart from differences in legal requirements, some practitioners have observed that common law contracts are lengthier because lawyers attempt to anticipate every possible scenario that might arise when a contract is performed. While it is difficult to generalize, some practitioners think that civil law contracts are usually shorter because the contract can simply refer to provisions from the code. However, even in civil law countries there is a trend toward longer contracts because the two systems often blend together when negotiations cross borders.

Key takeaway. At the beginning of any negotiation determine whether the contract is governed by a system of law that is different from the one with which you are familiar.

Type of Contract

The second variable relating to the source of contract law requires an understanding of the type of contract you are negotiating. For example, let's assume that you manufacture golf equipment. I am negotiating the purchase of 100 putters, which I want to sell in my store. We reach agreement on all details except price. Do we have a contract?

Under traditional common law, which governs the sale of real estate and services, price was a key element in forming a contract. However, our contract involves what lawyers call the sale of "goods." In the US, the sale of goods is governed by the Uniform Commercial Code or, as it is commonly called in business negotiations, the UCC. The UCC has modernized contract law. For example, even when the price is not settled, if you intend to form a contract but have said nothing about price, the UCC provides that "the price is a reasonable price at the time of delivery" of the putters.

The situation becomes more complicated if you are negotiating an international contract. The good news is that 81 countries, including the US, have ratified a treaty called the United Nations

Convention on Contracts for the International Sale of Goods (known in business circles as the CISG). Having a uniform international sales law is a tremendous achievement that facilitates international trade.

The bad news is that some of the rules in the CISG differ from the UCC. For example, some experts have concluded that under the CISG the price must be stated or the contract must include a provision for determining the price. (Miller, *Fundamentals of Business Law*)

Key takeaway. At the beginning of any negotiation, determine whether the contract involves the sale of goods, in which case the UCC will apply within the US and the CISG will apply if the contract involves businesses from two countries that have adopted this treaty (unless the parties agree otherwise).

USE A FOUR-PART CONTRACT CHECKLIST

We now turn to the four key legal elements necessary to create a contract. These elements in effect represent a checklist for use in your future negotiations.

1. Reach an Agreement

The requirement that parties reach an agreement is fairly straightforward. One party makes an offer; the other party accepts the offer.

In many cases, common sense dictates whether a contract has been formed, as illustrated by facts adapted from a case in China. Let's assume that on Monday a store sent an offer to purchase televisions to a manufacturer, with delivery to be made to the store. On Wednesday, the manufacturer sent a reply accepting the offer but added that the store had to pick up the televisions at the factory. On Friday, the store agreed to this change. When the price of televisions dropped, the store claimed that there was no contract. Is there a contract?

Monday: Offers to buy TVs; delivery to store

Store

Manufacturer

Wednesday: Accepts offer, but store to pick up at plant

Friday: Store says OK

A common sense analysis is that the store made an offer on Monday but the manufacturer's so-called "acceptance" was not a legal acceptance because it revised the terms of the offer by changing the place of delivery. This made the manufacturer's communication a counteroffer, which legally is a rejection of the offer. The counteroffer was accepted by the store on Friday, which created a contract. (For reasons too complicated to address here, under the UCC acceptance possibly occurred on Wednesday, but in any event there is a contract.)

Preliminary documents. A risky situation can arise when parties use a preliminary document during contract negotiations. This type of document (often called a memorandum of understanding, a memorandum of agreement, a letter of intent or an agreement in principle) is a useful negotiating tool in complex negotiations when the two sides have difficulty reducing their negotiated agreement to writing. Even in a simple negotiation, such as rental of an apartment, a pre-printed lease is a useful tool for converting a negotiation into a legal agreement.

Using preliminary documents carries a major risk. If the parties do not state clearly that they are not legally bound until a final contract is signed, as a document becomes more detailed a court might conclude that it has morphed into a binding contract.

This risk might also affect third parties. For example, several years ago Pennzoil negotiated a memorandum of agreement to acquire Getty Oil. When Texaco later entered into a separate contract to purchase Getty Oil, Pennzoil claimed that its memo-randum of agreement was actually a binding contract and that Texaco's actions interfered with Pennzoil's contract rights. In a subsequent trial, the jury agreed with Pennzoil in deciding that Texaco owed $10.5 billion in damages.

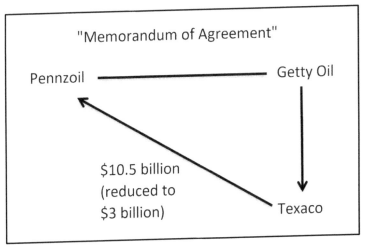

This was the largest verdict ever to be upheld on appeal. When this judgment drove Texaco into bankruptcy the two companies reached a settlement agreement whereby Texaco paid Pennzoil "only" $3 billion. The Pennzoil attorney later recounted that: "We celebrated that night [after winning the case] at my house by eating hamburgers and drinking beer. I've still got the $3 billion deposit slip on my wall." (*ABA Journal*, March 2, 2009)

Key takeaway. While preliminary agreements are useful negotiating tools, they also carry significant risks. To minimize these risks, you should carefully spell out in the document that it is for negotiating purposes only and is not a final contract until you so agree.

2. Give Up Something as Consideration

Consideration is a common law requirement. While consideration has a technical legal definition, in everyday language it means that for a deal to be legally binding, both sides must give up something. For example, if a graduate promises to donate $20 million to her university in a written signed agreement, the agreement is generally not binding unless the university promises to give up something in return.

In most business transactions consideration is not a concern because both sides promise to give up something. One side promises to provide a service or a product and the other side promises to make payment.

However, the risk of not meeting the consideration requirement increases when a contract is modified. Let's assume that you, as a contractor, promise to remodel a building for a customer by a certain date and the customer promises to pay you $30,000. The two promises represent your mutual consideration.

At your request, the customer promises in writing to give you a one-month extension, but you do not give the customer anything in exchange for this extension. Technically, the customer's agreement is not binding unless you provide additional consideration for the one-month extension.

Key takeaway. To create a binding contract or when you negotiate an amendment to a contract, make sure that both sides give up something to satisfy the consideration requirement.

3. Stay Within the Law

A contract that calls for the violation of a law is not enforceable. In many cases—for example, a contract to sell illegal drugs—this element is uncomplicated and easy to understand. In other situations, where there might be a violation of public policy, the law is more complex.

For instance, your company might decide to protect confidential information by adopting a policy that requires current employees to sign so-called "non-compete" agreements. These agreements state that the employees cannot work for a competitor within three years after leaving your company.

States differ on the legality and therefore the enforceability of these non-compete agreements. In some states these agreements might be illegal because they restrict the ability of your employees to obtain employment. Even where the agreement is legal, in common law countries the consideration element would require your company to give something to current employees in exchange for requiring them to sign the non-compete agreement.

Key takeaway. Illegal contracts are not enforceable, including contracts that violate public policy.

4. Put Your Agreement in Writing

Writing requirements raise important and complex concerns during negotiations. Both civil law and common law countries have rules providing that certain contracts must be in writing. Here are some typical examples under US law:

- Contracts for the sale of real estate

- Promises to pay the debts of others

- Agreements by an executor or administrator of an estate

- Promises made in exchange for a promise to marry

- Agreements that cannot be performed within one year

- Sales of goods for $500 or more

These rules carry a huge financial risk when you make a wrong assumption about whether your agreement must be in writing. For instance, you might miss a business opportunity because you thought that your oral agreement was binding in a situation where the law requires a written contract. Or you might create an unintended liability because you thought that your oral agreement was not binding in a situation where the contract did not legally have to be in writing.

As a result, you should never enter into a contract negotiation without understanding the rules about whether writing is required. Your understanding of the law should be supplemented by a practical strategy: During negotiations of important contracts make it clear that you are not bound until a written agreement is completed.

There are two reasons for this recommendation. First, by putting your agreement in writing you will not have to worry about the complex legal rules that determine whether the agreement must be written.

Second, and perhaps more important, you will avoid the consequences of memory failure. Even when the law allows oral contracts, the two sides to a contract will often have different recollections of the details of their negotiation and agreement. Their views might differ about when the agreement starts, how long it continues, how it can be terminated, and so on. These memory problems are avoided when you sign a written agreement. As noted by a Chinese proverb, even the palest ink is better than the best memory.

Parol Evidence Rule. A separate risk arises after you reduce your agreement to writing. To illustrate this risk, assume that you have just been hired by a company in a city distant from your own. During negotiations the company promises to pay for your moving costs but when the agreement is put into writing this promise is not included. Are you legally entitled to moving costs, assuming that the company admits it made the promise?

While the law varies from country to country, under the law of the United States and many other countries, the Parol Evidence Rule states that once you have put your agreement into writing, evidence of prior or contemporaneous agreements (such as the company's promise to pay you moving costs) cannot be used as evidence if you decide to sue the company.

This rule makes sense because during a negotiation both sides might make many agreements that they later cast aside and don't intend to include in the final contract. If they were allowed to bring evidence of these agreements into court, courts would forever be reviewing and attempting to untangle the details of what happened during the negotiations.

Even when you negotiate a deal under the laws of a country that has not adopted the Parol Evidence Rule, it is likely that your contract will include a provision stating that the rule applies. These provisions appear under a variety of headings—for example, merger clause, integration clause, or entire agreement clause.

It is good practice to include one of these provisions even when negotiating in countries that have adopted the rule because it might not apply in all situations. For example, the United States has adopted the Convention on Contracts for the International Sale of Goods (CISG), which does not include the rule. So if you enter into a contract for the international sale of goods governed by the CISG, evidence of prior agreements might be admissible in court unless you include a merger clause that clearly states that evidence outside the written contract is not admissible.

Here is an example of a typical contract provision (from the US Securities and Exchange Commission archives). In January, 2012, Facebook founder Mark Zuckerberg signed a contract amending an earlier employment agreement naming him as President and Chief Executive Officer of the company. The agreement contained the following standard provisions:

1. *Compensation.* Base wage of $500,000, along with bonus provision. (By the way, as of 2014, Zuckerberg was worth an estimated $33 billion. When the contract was signed he owned around 28% of Facebook stock.)
2. *Employee benefits.* Up to 21 days of paid time off per year.
3. *Confidentiality agreement.* Relates to a separate confidentiality and invention assignment agreement.
4. *No conflicting obligations.* Prohibits oral or written agreements that conflict with company policy.
5. *Outside activities.* No other business activity without the company's consent.
6. *Zuckerberg's general obligations.* Includes honesty, integrity, loyalty and professionalism.
7. *At-will employment.* Can be fired at any time.
8. *Withholdings.* Compensation is paid after subtraction of withholding payments.

The contract concluded with this sentence: "This letter agreement supercedes and replaces any prior understandings or agreements, whether oral, written or implied, between you and the Company regarding the matters described in this letter." Through this statement, Zuckerberg and Facebook have affirmed the Parol Evidence Rule.

Form of the writing. Contracts do not have to be printed in a formal document that says "Contract" at the top. Any writing will usually suffice—and this can be a trap. For example, two individuals were having some drinks at a restaurant. One of them, Lucy, offered to buy Zehmer's 472-acre farm for $50,000. Zehmer accepted the offer and wrote on a restaurant order form: "We hereby agree to sell to W.O. Lucy the Ferguson Farm complete for $50,000, title satisfactory to buyer." Zehmer and his wife signed the document.

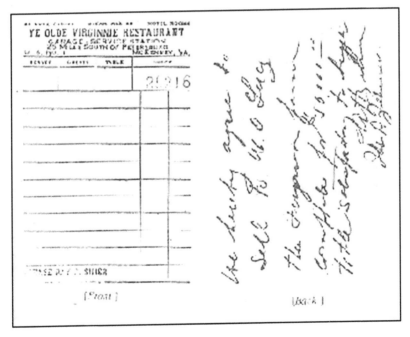

Zehmer later reneged on the agreement, claiming that he thought Lucy was kidding. He also argued that he "was as high as a Georgia pine" and that the negotiation was between "two doggoned drunks bluffing to see who could talk the biggest." In deciding that Zehmer had to give up his farm because this was a valid contract, the court emphasized a number of factors that indicated that this was intended to be a serious business transaction, including the appearance and completeness of the contract. (*Lucy v. Zehmer*, 84 S.E.2d 516)

Key takeaway. Even when a written contract is required, such as the sale of real estate, an informal written agreement can be just as binding as a formal document.

Implied terms. Whether or not your agreement is written, there might be additional terms implied by the law. For example, assume that you recently moved to the United States. Some friends want you to be the catcher on their baseball team. They tell you that the pitcher on the team throws a knuckleball pitch. You have never played baseball and have no idea what that means.

A local high school baseball coach is holding a garage sale and is selling some baseball gear. You visit the sale knowing that the seller is a baseball coach and tell him that you need a catcher's mitt that will catch knuckleballs. The coach points to a mitt while stating that it is the only catcher's mitt for sale. You then negotiate a price. After buying the mitt, you discover that it is much too small to catch knuckleballs. Can you sue the coach for breach of contract?

Although you never discussed it during the negotiation, the Uniform Commercial Code (the law governing the sale of goods) provides that in these circumstances a seller like the coach gives you an implied warranty that the item sold is fit for the particular purpose for which you need the product, here catching knuckleballs. The coach is in breach of this implied warranty.

Key takeaway. Keep in mind that your agreement might include terms that are implied by law, even if they were never discussed during the negotiation.

9 Move Beyond Legalities to Create Value

As noted in Chapter 8, a contract is defined as an agreement enforceable by law. Business contracts are typically designed to be *value-creating* agreements enforceable by law. For example, when you enter into a contract with a supplier, you anticipate that the supplier's product will enable you to increase the value of your own products.

Lawyers traditionally have focused on the enforceability part of the contract definition; their goal is to construct legally perfect, enforceable agreements that minimize legal risk. The lawyers' orientation is not surprising given their mindset. Lawyers are trained to look at contracts through the eyes of a judge who might eventually have to rule on a contract dispute. Thus a good contract, from the lawyers' perspective, is one that minimizes the client's risk and is enforceable in court.

While the "enforceable by law" part of the business contract definition is important and cannot be ignored, legal enforceability must be balanced with the "value-creating agreement" part of the definition. In other words, while businesses want their agreements to be enforceable, they also want contracts that enable them to achieve their business goals. They view the contract as a management tool as well as a legal tool. As law professors Ian Macneil and Paul Gudel note in their book *Contracts: Exchange Transactions and Relations*, "[o]nly lawyers and other trouble-oriented folk look on contracts primarily as a source of trouble and disputation, rather than a way of getting things done."

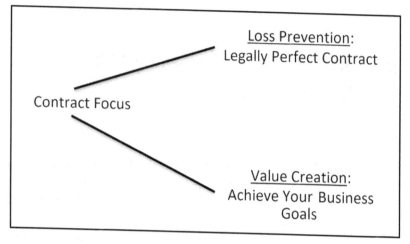

This chapter focuses on two approaches that can be used to reconcile the tension between business and legal objectives of a contract: A lean contracting strategy that reshapes the content of contracts, and visualization, which is designed to make legal concepts more understandable.

Simplify Your Contracts Through Lean Contracting

A lean contracting strategy might enable managers, along with their lawyers, to refocus on value creation by minimizing legal complexity in their contracts. This strategy applies lean production concepts to the "production" of contracts by asking whether company contracts can be simplified through an examination of the costs and benefits of various contract clauses.

For example, the in-house legal team at the brewing company Scottish & Newcastle sensed that company resources were being wasted in the contract negotiation process. Their work in developing what they call the Pathclearer approach to commercial contracting—which is a form of lean contracting—illustrates the benefits that are possible from reorienting contracting strategy. Unless otherwise noted, the quotations in this chapter regarding this approach are from a highly-recommended article by Weatherley entitled "Pathclearer—A more commercial approach to drafting commercial contracts" (*PLC Law Department Quarterly*, October–December, 2005).

Purpose of a contract. The lawyers initially asked three fundamental questions. First, what is the purpose of a contract? In answering this question, they used a traditional definition of a legal contract:

> [T]he only purpose of a contract . . . is to ensure that rights and obligations which the parties agree to can be enforced in court (or arbitration). Put even more bluntly, the essence of a contract is the ability to force someone else to do something they don't want to do, or to obtain compensation for their failure.

With this definition in mind, they realized that certain terms, such as product specifications, should always be in writing and that certain types of deals, such as "share purchases, loan agreements, and guarantees," require detailed written contracts.

But they also realized that many other scenarios—for instance, a long-term relationship between a customer and supplier—call for a "much lighter legal touch." They recognized that in these situations the consequences of forcing contractual obligations on an unwilling partner through "begrudging performance" or litigation are not attractive.

They concluded that leaving long-term relationships to "free market economics [is better than an] attempt to place continuing contractual obligations on each other." In other words, freedom of the market should dominate the traditional freedom of contract philosophy that has led to detailed written contracts.

Drawbacks of traditional detailed contracts. The second of the lawyers' three fundamental questions focused on the risks associated with traditional, law-oriented contracts: "What are the drawbacks of detailed written contracts?" In answering this question, the in-house lawyers reached six insightful conclusions.

1. *Illusory and costly attempts to reach certainty.* "The apparent certainty and protection of a detailed written contract . . . [are] often illusory" and wasteful as companies pay their lawyers first for drafting contracts that only the lawyers understand and second for interpreting what the contracts mean.

   The in-house legal team witnessed "bizarre attempts" by lawyers attempting to reach certainty. For example, external lawyers spent "hours drafting and debating the precise legal definition of beer for insertion in a simple beer supply agreement." The legal team also recognized the futility of trying to predict the future.

2. *Dispute resolution.* Detailed contracts can result in legalistic dispute resolution.

   > Without a detailed contract, business people who become involved in a dispute will generally discuss the issue and reach a sensible agreement on how to resolve it . . . . However, where a detailed contract exists, the same parties will feel obliged to consult their lawyers.

   This conclusion brings to mind my recent conversation with a CEO. In his opinion, the only purpose of a contract is, as he put it, to "give a right to sue." When disputes arose between his company and its customers he advised his staff to ignore the contract and work out a solution that met the customers' needs.

3. *Complexity*. The complexity of contracts causes confusion and creates a risk that the parties will be unable to focus on key terms because it becomes "difficult to see the wood for the trees."

4. *Unnecessary terms*. The general law of contracts provides "a fair middle-ground solution to most issues" and "[t]he beauty of simply relying on the 'general law,' rather than trying to set out the commercial arrangement in full in a detailed written contract, is that there is no need to negotiate the non-key terms of a deal."

5. *Expense*. Negotiating detailed written contracts is expensive in terms of management time, lawyer time and delayed business opportunities.

6. *Wrong focus*. Detailed written contracts can cause the parties to focus on worst-case scenarios that "can lead to the souring of relationships . . . . [C]ontinuing business relationships are like butterflies. They are subtle and hard to capture. When you do try to nail them down, you can kill them in the process."

The lawyers might have added to this list the concerns that arise when negotiating with individuals from other cultures. As discussed in Chapter 5, in countries like China developing a relationship with someone you trust is more important than trying to cover all contingencies in a lengthy contract.

Surveys by a leading international association of contract negotiators, the International Association for Contract & Commercial Management (IACCM), confirm the insights of the Scottish lawyers. IACCM conducts an annual survey of thousands of its members (from both common law and civil law countries) to determine the contract terms that are most negotiated and the terms that are most important. Surprisingly, there is a disconnect between the results. For example, the top five "most negotiated" terms in recent years (2009 to 2013/2014) are:

1. Limitation of Liability
2. Price/Charge/Price Changes
3. Indemnification
4. Intellectual Property
5. Payment

None of these terms are on the latest (2013/2014) list of "most important" terms:

1. Scope and Goals
2. Responsibilities of the parties
3. Change management
4. Delivery/Acceptance
5. Communications & Reporting

A report on the survey results (*2013/2014 Top Terms*) concluded that:

> [M]ost business-to-business negotiations are dominated by discussions over financial issues (price and payment) and risk allocation (liabilities, indemnities, data security, performance undertakings and liquidated damages) . . . . [T]hey do not contribute to the win-win approach that negotiators claim they prefer. In past surveys, almost 80% of participants acknowledge that the focus of their negotiations do not result in the best outcome for either party.

Other ways to achieve business goals. The third and final question the in-house legal team asked is whether there are other ways to achieve business goals without detailed written contracts. The Scottish & Newcastle lawyers answered this question in the affirmative by focusing on the concept of "commercial affinity."

Commercial affinity is the force that keeps parties together in "mutually beneficial commercial relationships." The alignment of the parties' interests through carefully- constructed incentives, combined with the right of either side to walk away from the deal if it ceases to be economically attractive, incentivizes them to meet the other side's needs and alleviates the need for "a myriad of tactical rights and obligations in a contract."

In summary, the Scottish & Newcastle lawyers realized that a different approach is appropriate "when the parties are in a continuing business relationship, rather than just carrying out a snapshot transaction" that might require a detailed written contract. They do not advocate a complete return to handshake agreements. For instance, "exit arrangements (such as obligations to buy dedicated assets from the supplier . . .) do need to be spelled out in the contract." But by addressing the three fundamental questions, they realized that in many other situations leaner contracts were possible.

The company's Pathclearer approach in a continuing business relationship is illustrated by the lean contract that the company negotiated with a service provider. The two parties originally had a ten-year contract that ran over 200 pages. During contract renegotiation they substantially reduced the size of the contract through the Pathclearer approach by giving each party the right to terminate after 12 months' notice—a mutual "nuclear button."

> By giving ourselves the ability to terminate at any time, we avoided the need to have to negotiate detailed terms in the contract . . . . This is a much more powerful way of influencing the service provider than a technical debate over whether they were complying with the words set out in the contract.

The following figure illustrates a contract between a US beer company and one of its suppliers—23 pages plus 8 pages of exhibits.

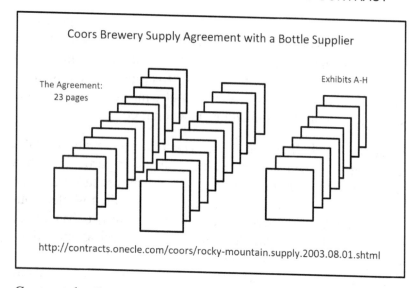

Contrast the Coors contract with a Pathclearer contract with one of its suppliers—one page plus one attachment.

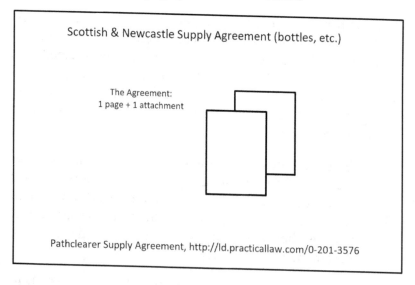

Use Visualization to Understand Your Negotiations and Contracts

As the contract diagrams illustrate, a picture can be worth a thousand words. Using pictures and other forms of visualization can help you clarify your negotiation decisions and better understand the terms of the contract you are negotiating.

Visualizing negotiation decisions. In making your contracts leaner, you might be able to eliminate or soften certain provisions that cause expensive contract negotiations. Visualization can help you identify these provisions.

For example, an indemnity clause in Microsoft's contracts caused many contract negotiations to last an additional 60 to 90 days because customers did not want to provide the indemnity requested by Microsoft. Microsoft softened the provision after realizing that the benefits of the clause were minimal in contrast to potential costs such as reputational costs (resulting from confrontational negotiations), resource costs (lawyer and management time) and cash flow costs (caused by delayed sales during the additional two to three months of contract negotiation).

In describing and commenting on these costs, Tim Cummins, CEO of IACCM, concluded that "[r]isk management is about balancing consequence and probability. Here is an example where consequence was managed without regard to probability—and as a result, other risks and exposures [such as reputational and resource costs] became inevitable." ("Best practices in commercial contracting," in the book *A Proactive Approach*)

Decision trees, which were discussed in Chapter 3, are useful in visualizing negotiation decisions that balance risk and probability like the one that Microsoft faced. Let's assume that the contract clause in question provided Microsoft with $20 million in indemnity and there is a 1% chance that the company will lose $20 million and invoke the clause. (This probability can be estimated on the basis of past experience. In practice, the chance that such a clause would be invoked is probably less than 1%.)

Let's also assume that management and lawyer time to negotiate the indemnity and cash flow costs resulting from delayed sales during negotiations total $1 million. In effect, Microsoft would pay $1 million for the equivalent of a $20 million insurance policy. Given these assumptions, should Microsoft pay $1 million for this "insurance"?

The following decision tree depicts the 1 percent chance that Microsoft will lose $20 million if it drops the indemnification clause demand and the 99 percent chance that it will lose nothing. This results in an expected value of –$200,000 (0.99 × 0 plus 0.01 × $2 million). Based on these assumed values and probabilities (and not factoring in its attitude toward risk), Microsoft made a wise decision when it softened its negotiating stance.

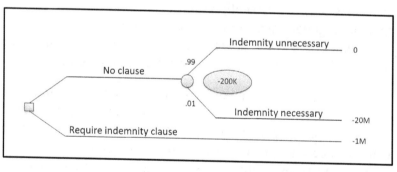

In this case, we made an assumption that Microsoft's negotiation costs were $1 million. Sometimes the lost opportunities relating to slow negotiations are much higher. For instance, a prominent oil and gas attorney told me that he represented a company that negotiated the sale of property to a buyer for $30 million. Signing the contract was delayed when the buyer's law firm insisted on a clause that immunized the buyer from a low-probability event. While negotiations over this clause were in process, another buyer offered to pay over $100 million for the property. The law firm's desire for a perfect legal contract cost the client over $70 million!

Visualizing contract provisions and other legal documents. Visualization can also help you understand the terms in a contract and in other legal complex documents. For example, contracts are often filled with clauses like the following that challenge the cognitive skills of negotiators:

> This Agreement shall be valid for an initial period of three (3) years from the date of signing. Unless either Party gives notice of termination at least six (6) months before the expiry of the three-year period, it shall remain in force until further notice, with a notice period of at least three (3) months. Notice shall be given in writing.

> (Adapted from Ruuki's *Framework Agreement for Purchasing Services*)

In the following diagram, leaders in the visualization movement Stefania Passera and Helena Haapio (my frequent co-author) show how visualization can clarify the meaning of this clause.

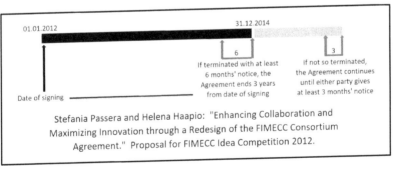

Stefania Passera and Helena Haapio: "Enhancing Collaboration and Maximizing Innovation through a Redesign of the FIMECC Consortium Agreement." Proposal for FIMECC Idea Competition 2012.

Another example illustrates the value of using visualization when dealing with other forms of complex legal documents. In 2013, Helena Haapio invited me to a Legal Design Jam, a design hackathon to visualize the Wikimedia Foundation trademark policy. She was a facilitator, along with Stefania Passera, Margaret Hagen from Stanford, and Yana Welinder, Legal Counsel for the Foundation. The small group of participants included a mixture of designers and attorneys.

Before the redesign effort, the trademark policy was a typical densely-worded legal document. The end result of the Legal Design Jam was a revised policy that is colorful and clear: http://wikimediafoundation.org/wiki/Trademark_policy.

At this website, a green checkmark is used to denote situations where users can freely use marks, such as when they are used to discuss Wikimedia sites in literary works. An orange question mark is used in situations where permission is required (such as when you want "to use the Wikipedia logo in a movie") and a red "x" indicates uses that are prohibited (for example, when you create a website that mimics a Wikimedia site).

Key takeaway. The use of visualization through decision trees, pictures, diagrams and color can clarify your negotiation decisions and your understanding of complex legal documents.

IV COMPLETE YOUR END GAME

10. Perform and Evaluate Your Agreement

10   Perform and Evaluate Your Agreement

Most contracts are undoubtedly performed without unusual complications. Our focus in this chapter is on situations where there are performance difficulties. The chapter emphasizes alternatives to litigation that are designed to keep you and the other side out of court. As noted in Chapter 2, these alternatives fall under the collective heading of "alternative dispute resolution" (ADR).

Understanding ADR processes is important for three reasons. First, as part of a business negotiation you must decide whether to include discussion of ADR in your contract negotiations. To understand what you are negotiating, you should understand the basics of the two key ADR processes, mediation and arbitration.

Even when your attorney is involved in the negotiations, you might have to take the lead in negotiating ADR clauses. According to one study, around one-third of attorneys "never advised their clients to try mediation or arbitration." ("Attorneys' Use of ADR is Crucial to Their Willingness to Recommend It to Clients," *Dispute Resolution Magazine*, Winter 2000) This is what legendary litigator Joe Jamail had to say about mediation: "I'm a trial lawyer . . . . There are some lawyers who do nothing but this mediation bull****. Do you know what the root of mediation is? Mediocrity!" ("Lions of the Trial Bar," *ABA Journal*, March 2009)

On the other hand, many lawyers are enthusiastic about ADR. Perhaps Gandhi said it best:

> My joy was boundless. I had learned the true practice of law. I had learned to find out the better side of human nature and to enter men's hearts. I realized that the true function of a lawyer was to unite parties . . . . The lesson was so indelibly burnt into me that a large part of my time during the last 20 years of my practice as a lawyer was occupied in bringing about private compromises of hundreds of cases. I lost nothing thereby—not even money, certainly not my soul.
>
> (Gandhi, *An Autobiography: The Story of My Experiments With Truth*)

The second reason why an understanding of ADR processes is important is that you might become a participant in these processes if a dispute arises over performance of a contract. If you have agreed to arbitration, you will participate in the selection of the arbitrator, you must decide whether you need an attorney, you should understand whether you can appeal the arbitrator's decision, and so on.

Third, in the course of your business and personal life you will often play the role of a third party as you resolve work disputes or family disputes. At a minimum, you should be able to make an informed decision about whether it is better to act as an arbitrator or whether a mediator role makes more sense.

This chapter opens with a topic that is sometimes overlooked in discussion of ADR: dispute prevention. We then turn to the two key ADR processes—arbitration and mediation—along with a discussion of ADR tools you can use to implement these processes. The chapter concludes by examining concepts designed to help you review, evaluate and improve your negotiations.

PREVENT DISPUTES

Dispute prevention focuses on predicting what people do rather than on what courts might decide. In the words of Professor Edward Dauer: "The first principle of preventive law is that it is often more important to predict what people will do than to predict what a court will do." (*Corporate Dispute Management*) One rationale for this principle was painfully stated by the French philosopher Voltaire: "I was never ruined but twice: once when I lost a lawsuit and once when I won one."

I had first-hand experience with dispute prevention several years ago after spending a night at a Marriott hotel in Texas. I was scheduled to give a legal briefing to a group of corporate executives the following morning and asked the front desk for a wake-up call. The call never came.

When checking out, I mentioned the missing call when completing a feedback card. A couple of weeks later, the President of Marriott, Bill Marriott, sent a personal note to my home in Stanford, California, where I was teaching at the time. In the note, he apologized for the missed call and mentioned that he had asked the hotel general manager to investigate the matter.

Another hotel adopted a different approach following a well-publicized, tragic incident. International recording star Connie Francis was raped by an intruder while staying at a Howard Johnson Motor Lodge. Her reaction: "I never received so much as a note from Mr. Howard B. Johnson saying 'We're sorry it happened.' After being shocked, I was very angry." (*New York Times*, July 2, 1976) After becoming angry, she sued the hotel and eventually won $2.5 million.

We can only speculate why the hotel never communicated with Connie Francis. Probably the company leaders followed the traditional approach by asking their lawyers whether a court might hold them liable—focusing on what a court might do. The attorneys might have responded that the hotel should not be held liable for the acts of an independent third party (at least under the law at the time) and they might have gone further by advising company management not to contact the singer or do anything else that might indicate that it was liable. This was the traditional approach, which is in sharp contrast to the Marriott apology.

The two examples illustrate situations where hotels did (Marriott) and did not (Howard Johnson) use a preventive law approach *after* a problem developed. You can also incorporate a preventive approach into your contracts before incidents arise. For example, a process called "partnering" is used in the construction industry. While there are many variations, this is the usual format, as described in *The Construction Industry's Guide to Dispute Avoidance and Resolution* published by the American Arbitration Association (AAA).

> [R]epresentatives of the project's stakeholders attend pre-construction workshops in order to get to know each other and share concerns. Neutral facilitators guide discussions about the project, specific individual goals and agendas. It is during these meetings that participants develop ways to recognize risks that may create obstacles to the success of the project. They develop methods to avoid, control or cope with potential sources of conflict. The eventual outcome is a joint agreement signed by the workshop participants that sets forth their goals and expresses their commitment to the project.

Key takeaway. During negotiations, consider adding a dispute prevention clause to your contracts.

USE ARBITRATION TO RESOLVE YOUR CONTRACT DISPUTES

We now turn to the first of two basic ADR processes—arbitration. Agreements to resolve disputes through arbitration permeate our personal lives. If you use a credit card, have automobile insurance, buy stock, use eBay or use Amazon, you probably have agreed to arbitrate your disputes. For example, my (and your) arbitration agreement with Amazon provides:

> Any dispute or claim relating in any way to your use of any Amazon Service, or to any products or services sold or distributed by Amazon or through Amazon.com will be resolved by binding arbitration, rather than in court . . . . There is no judge or jury in arbitration, and court review of an arbitration award is limited.

Beyond consumer agreements, arbitration is a common business dispute resolution process and is even used to resolve disputes with governments. In 2014, an international arbitration tribunal decided that Russia owes $50 billion to the shareholders of Yukos as compensation for company assets that were seized. ("Now Try Collecting," *The Economist*, August 2, 2014)

The Arbitration Process

The arbitration process generally follows this sequence, as noted in *A Guide to Mediation and Arbitration for Business People* (AAA).

Agreement. In most situations arbitration is not used unless you first agree to the process. You can agree when you first enter into a contract, as in the Amazon example, or you can agree after a dispute arises.

Selecting an arbitrator. Your agreement might provide that an arbitration service, such as the American Arbitration Association, will provide a list of potential arbitrators from a roster it maintains. If you and the other side cannot agree on an arbitrator from the list, the service can name one for you.

You can also use a more informal approach when selecting an arbitrator. For example, if you are creating a partnership with another person, you could provide in your agreement that if a dispute arises each of you will appoint an arbitrator and these two arbitrators will then select a third arbitrator.

Hearing and award. The arbitration hearing is much like a trial in court and you must decide whether to be represented by an attorney. The arbitrator has the power to subpoena witnesses if necessary. The hearing will begin with an opening statement, followed by examination and cross-examination of witnesses and a closing statement.

Unlike litigation, the hearing is private and the arbitrator will normally use common sense rather than technical rules of court procedure in deciding what evidence is relevant to the case.

Following the hearing, the arbitrator will reach a decision. Although not always the case, the arbitrator might make the decision without providing an opinion that explains the rationale for the decision. If the losing party does not comply with the award, the decision can be enforced by a court.

Appeals

Because public policy favors the finality of arbitration awards, the ability to appeal an award using the court system is limited. While courts might overturn an award when, for example, the arbitrator is engaged in corruption or fraud, they will usually not intervene even when the arbitrator makes a mistake regarding the facts or the law.

This rule of finality was cited by a California court in *Palo Alto v. Service Employees International Union* (91 Cal. Rptr.2d 500). A City of Palo Alto employee threatened other employees with physical violence and even threatened to shoot them. The employees treated the threats as jokes. The employee also said that he could kill someone while 600 yards away. He owned 18 rifles and pistols and had a personalized license plate that read "SHOOOT."

Following a dispute, the employee in question threatened to shoot another employee and that employee's wife and baby. This led to an arrest for making a terrorist threat and he eventually pleaded guilty to disturbing the peace. The City also obtained an injunction that prohibited the employee from having any contact with the person he threatened and decided to terminate his employment.

The City's decision then went to an arbitrator as allowed under a union contract. The arbitrator decided, among other things, that the threats were "everyday 'boy talk'" that were tolerated at this workplace and were not genuine. As a result, he ordered reinstatement of the employee to his position and awarded him back pay.

On appeal, the court quoted precedent that "judicial review of arbitration awards is extremely narrow" and that "an arbitrator's decision is not generally reviewable for errors of fact or law [even when it] causes substantial injustice to the parties." (However, in an unusual twist, the court eventually decided that the employee could not be reinstated in this case because of the earlier injunction.)

If you want to use arbitration but are concerned about placing too much power in the hands of an arbitrator whose decision cannot be appealed, you can try to negotiate an agreement that includes an appeals process. For instance, effective November 2013, the American Arbitration Association adopted rules permitting an appeal to a panel of arbitrators that is allowed to review "errors of law that are material and prejudicial, and determinations of fact that are clearly erroneous." (AAA, *Optional Appellate Arbitration Rules*)

Understand the Costs of Arbitration

Negotiators often attempt to include arbitration agreements in contracts because of perceived cost savings. However, certain aspects of arbitration might be more expensive than litigation. Based on cost estimates from experts in Texas, Florida and Pennsylvania, the arbitration of a $600,000 construction dispute would cost $25,400 for the filing fee, case service, and compensation for the arbitrator. The comparable litigation cost would total $300 for a filing fee (since the case service, judge and courtroom are free).

However, the total legal costs would be $120,300 as compared to $94,500 for arbitration. One reason is that legal fees for litigation are much higher. Legal fees for preparing for and attending the trial alone are $12,000 higher than for attending an arbitration hearing. And an appeal of the court decision would add substantially to the cost differential. ("Comparing Cost in Construction Arbitration & Litigation," *Dispute Resolution Journal*, May/July 2007)

Key takeaway. Keep in mind two important factors when deciding whether to negotiate to include an arbitration clause in your contracts. First, in most cases, appeal of the arbitrator's decision will not be allowed, with the result that the arbitrator will be your judge, jury and court of appeals. Second, arbitration proceedings might not be as economical as commonly thought, but are probably still cheaper than litigation.

USE MEDIATION TO RESOLVE YOUR CONTRACT DISPUTES

Types of Mediation

Mediation is the second of the two basic ADR processes. In essence, mediation is a negotiation assisted by a third party. Traditionally, the goal of mediation was to solve a specific problem using one of two mediation processes. In the first process, facilitative mediation, the mediator's role is to make it easier for the parties to discuss and resolve their concerns. In the second process, evaluative mediation, the mediator is also asked to evaluate the merits of each side's case without making a decision (unlike arbitration).

In recent years a third option has developed—transformative mediation. While transformative mediation might also result in solving a specific problem, the ultimate goal is to improve the relationship between the parties. After the US Postal Service adopted transformative mediation in the 1990s, it saved millions of dollars in legal costs and productivity improvements. ("Companies Adopting Postal Service Grievance Process," *New York Times*, September 6, 2000)

I once asked someone who had researched mediation at the Postal Service for an example of transformation mediation. She mentioned a letter carrier who had filed a sexual harassment claim against her supervisor. Through transformative mediation, the parties discovered that the real problem was their relationship. The supervisor referred to the letter carrier and other letter carriers by their route numbers; the postal worker felt that this was dehumanizing. Once the relationship was fixed and the supervisor started referring to the letter carrier personally, the complaint was withdrawn.

121

The Caucus

One especially effective tool used by many mediators is the caucus. With a caucus, the mediator meets separately with each side to discuss their interests and positions. The mediator keeps this information confidential if the parties so desire.

Through this process the mediator can complete a negotiation analysis that includes each side's reservation price, "most likely" estimate, BATNA (best alternative to a negotiated agreement) and ZOPA (zone of potential agreement). The mediator can then either help the parties reach agreement within that zone or, if there is no zone, advise them that the mediation is a waste of time.

Key takeaway. Keep in mind that there are three types of mediation. Select a mediator whose abilities match the process that you have selected.

BE CREATIVE IN USING ADR PROCESSES

The two basic models of dispute resolution—arbitration and mediation—provide many opportunities for creativity and innovation. In one case at the outer limits of creativity, a judge, apparently fed up with the parties' reliance on the federal courts, decided to "fashion a new form of alternative dispute resolution, to wit: at 4:00 p.m. on Friday, June 30, 2006, counsel shall convene at a neutral site . . . . [and] shall engage in one game of 'rock, paper, scissors" to determine who wins a motion. (*Avista Management v. Wausau Underwriters*, 2006 AMC 1569)

The mini-trial and rent-a-judge are two prominent examples of mediation and arbitration variations.

Mini-Trial

The mini-trial is a variation of the mediation model. The prototypical mini-trial involved a $6 million intellectual property lawsuit filed by Telecredit against TRW. This lawsuit began much like any other. The parties spent around $500,000 and exchanged 100,000 documents, with no resolution in sight. Given the slow pace of the litigation, executives from the two companies created a structured process that came to be known as a mini-trial.

The process essentially involved five parties: one attorney and one executive from each side and a neutral expert on intellectual property. The attorneys each had a half day to explain their respective versions of the case and to answer questions from the executives. The executives then met briefly and resolved the case.

The estimated savings in legal fees was around $1 million. Through this process the executives were able to hear the case as presented by the other side's attorney (which might have been quite different from what they heard up to that point from their own attorneys). They were also able to resolve the case in a way that made business sense, as opposed to a typical court decision that produces a zero sum result (with one side winning and the other side losing $6 million in this case).

Rent-A-Judge

Rent-a-judge is a variation of the arbitration model. Although the hearing is similar to a trial, rent-a-judge offers the same benefits as other forms of arbitration. When Brad Pitt and Jennifer Anniston used rent-a-judge to handle their divorce in 2005, they were able to select their own judge (presumably a judge who was familiar with divorce proceedings). They were also able to conclude the divorce proceeding quickly and they maintained their privacy because the press was not allowed to attend the hearing. For further information, see: http://www.npr.org/tem

plates/story/story.php?storyId=4812658.

Use ADR for Deal Making

Historically, processes like arbitration and mediation have been used as alternatives to litigation for resolving disputes. However, in recent years these processes have also been increasingly used to negotiate deals. Mediation is especially promising because the use of a caucus enables mediators to prepare a negotiation analysis that takes into account confidential information from each side.

According to one study, close to 40% of the mediators surveyed had used mediation for deals ranging from $100,000 to $26 million. Examples of the deals included negotiations involving angel investments, physician partnerships, the sale of cable TV rights, and a software joint venture. (http://www.pon.harvard .edu/daily/mediation/mediation-in-transactional-negotiation-2/)

Arbitration is also a possibility for resolving difficult issues during negotiations. Baseball arbitration is a highly-publicized example that is used when players are involved in salary disputes with their teams. The unique feature of baseball arbitration is that each side submits a final figure to the arbitrator, who then must select one of the two figures.

For example, assume that a deadlock arises during negotiations in which Pitcher demands a salary of $20 million and Team offers $10 million. If they use the baseball form of arbitration, Pitcher and Team would privately submit salary figures to the arbitrator, who must select one of the two numbers. Wanting the arbitrator to select their number, each side is likely to be more reasonable than when making the original demands. While commonly used to facilitate baseball negotiations, this form of arbitration could be used in any type of deal-making negotiation.

Key takeaway. Think creatively when developing an ADR process. Consider using ADR processes for deal making.

USE FOUR KEY ADR TOOLS

Four ADR tools are especially useful in connection with business disputes: a corporate pledge, screens, contract clauses, and online resources.

Corporate Pledge

The International Institute for Conflict Prevention & Resolution (CPR) was a pioneer in the development of a pledge that companies can adopt as a statement of their corporate policy. The key sentence in the pledge states: "In the event of a business dispute between our company and another company which has made or will then make a similar statement, we are prepared to explore with that other party resolution of the dispute through negotiation or ADR techniques before pursuing full-scale litigation." Over 4,000 operating companies have adopted this policy. (http://www.cpradr.org/Home.aspx)

This pledge is especially useful given the tendency toward reactive devaluation discussed in Chapter 7. If you are involved in a dispute and propose an ADR process, the other side might react to the proposal by devaluing it, perhaps thinking that the proposal is a sign of weakness. This reaction might be diminished if you state that the proposal is the result of a preexisting corporate policy that favors ADR.

Screens

Screens are a series of questions designed to help parties select a binding or non-binding form of dispute resolution. Binding processes are arbitration and litigation; non-binding processes are mediation and negotiation.

CPR publishes an especially useful *ADR Suitability Guide* that features a mediation screen. In helping the disputing parties decide whether to use mediation, the screen asks questions that focus on the following factors, among others:

- The parties' relationship

- Importance of control over the process and decision

- Importance of discovery

- Chances for success in court

- Cost of litigation

- Importance of speed and privacy

- Relative power of both sides

Contract Clauses

Parties can enter into an ADR contract as part of the initial business negotiation before a dispute arises or they can wait until after a dispute develops. Post-dispute agreements are often difficult to negotiate because the relationship of the parties has soured. Here is an example of a pre-dispute agreement, which is part of Oracle's letter offering Mark Hurd the position of President:

> You and Oracle understand and agree that any existing or future dispute or claim arising out of or related to your Oracle employment, or the termination of that employment, will be resolved by final and binding arbitration and that no other forum for dispute resolution will be available to either party, except as to those claims identified below. The decision of the arbitrator shall be final and binding on both you and Oracle and it shall be enforceable by any court having proper jurisdiction.

> (http://contracts.onecle.com/oracle/hurd-offer-2010-09-

02.shtml)

ADR contract clauses might provide for only one process, like the Hurd arbitration clause, or the processes can be linked. For example, the parties might agree to use negotiation and/or mediation before turning to arbitration.

Online Dispute Resolution (ODR)

In recent years advances in technology have enabled ADR to become ODR. Online systems enable parties to use negotiation, mediation and arbitration to resolve business and personal disputes.

Your decision to use online dispute resolution involves a cost-benefit analysis. On one hand, online processes save travel costs and are convenient. On the other hand, there is evidence that they are less effective—especially because it is difficult to build a relationship with the other side. (As noted in Chapter 5, getting to know the other side is an especially important aspect of negotiation.) One way to surmount this problem is to combine face-to-face negotiation with online ODR by scheduling face time at the outset of the negotiation before moving to the online phase.

Key takeaway. When implementing ADR processes, use the four tools described in this section: the policy statement, screens, contract clauses and ODR.

REVIEW AND EVALUATE YOUR NEGOTIATION

Contracting is a key corporate capability that lies at the heart of value creation and competitive advantage. It is unlikely that any business can survive, let alone prosper, without financially successful contracts. Given the importance of contracts to company success, evaluation of negotiation and contract performance is essential.

The ultimate question during an evaluation is whether the contract was performed successfully. While many factors play a role in determining successful contract performance, the negotiation process is among the most important. This section provides suggestions for review of this process.

Conduct a General Review of the Negotiation

In conducting a post-negotiation review, you might be tempted to focus on where the negotiators spent most of their time instead of where their time should have been spent. As noted in Chapter 9, surveys by the International Association for Contract & Commercial Management (IACCM) concluded that the "most negotiated" contract terms are not the "most important." Instead of focusing your review on "most negotiated" terms (like limitation of liability, indemnification, and payment) spend more time on the "most important" terms (like scope and goals, the parties' responsibilities, and change management).

In addition to shifting your focus from "most negotiated" to "most important," ask whether you are using the correct measures of success and whether these measures are linked to the incentives of the negotiators within your organization. Both of these concerns are discussed in depth in an outstanding article by Danny Ertel in the *Harvard Business Review* entitled "Turning Negotiation into a Corporate Capability."

Ertel notes that on the buy side, instead of linking incentives to price discounts obtained by buyers, creative companies focus on "the operating efficiencies gained through using the supplier, the reductions in defects achieved by the supplier, and even the supplier's role in developing product or service innovations." On the sell side, incentives could be tied to the length of customer relationships with the company, innovations from these relationships, and referral business that comes from customers.

Identify Tension Between Deal Making and Implementation

In addition to your general review of negotiations, one aspect of contract negotiation and performance deserves special attention. Separation of deal makers from those responsible for implementation sometimes creates tension that affects performance of the contract.

For example, a large international consulting firm noticed that its implementation teams had to spend considerable time renegotiating contracts made by deal makers. They asked me to conduct a seminar in Paris in the springtime on how to renegotiate contracts. Hearing the words "Paris" and "springtime" I quickly agreed to conduct the seminar before realizing that I might have little to offer because a contract renegotiation basically follows the same principles as any contract negotiation.

So I decided to dig deeper by contacting the firm's leaders to find out *why* there were so many renegotiations. The reason for the renegotiations was best summarized by the response from one of the leaders, who noted that incentives of the individuals tasked with negotiating the deals were "more linked to closure [of the negotiation] than to ongoing implementation." With this information in hand, I was able to refocus the seminar on resolving the tension between deal making and deal implementation.

Danny Ertel has published an excellent article on this topic in the *Harvard Business Review* entitled "Getting Past Yes: Negotiating as if Implementation Mattered." In this article he notes that when business development teams become separated from implementation, they "are likely to focus more on the agreement than on its business impact."

In reviewing your negotiations, ask whether a deal making mindset dominates your organization's negotiations. Examples of this mindset from the Ertel article include using surprise to gain advantage, withholding information, using tactics such as false deadlines, and protecting yourself with penalty clauses.

Contrast this mindset with an implementation mindset that emphasizes, as Ertel points out, raising issues as soon as possible during negotiations, sharing information, spending as much time as necessary to develop an agreement that can be implemented successfully, and developing realistic commitments. Following your negotiation review, your goal should be to move toward an implementation focus.

Complete a Personal Review

Just as important as a company review of negotiations is a personal assessment of your negotiation strategy and tactics, with an eye toward continuing improvement. Here are some questions to ask during this assessment, based on material covered in this book.

- Did I establish a relationship with the other side?

- Did we search for underlying interests and find interests that aren't in conflict?

- Did I ask questions and listen carefully to the answers?

- Did I find out at the beginning of the negotiation whether the other side had authority to do a deal?

- Did I use an effective "first price" strategy?

- Did I look at the negotiation from the other side's perspective?

- Did I use reciprocity?

- Did I maintain a "big picture" outlook?

Key takeaway. Whether or not your organization conducts systematic reviews of contract negotiations and performance, you should conduct a personal assessment of your negotiation strategy and tactics to use as the basis for improvement.

A CLOSING PERSPECTIVE: THE LIFE GOALS ANALYSIS

A few years ago I gave a presentation on dispute resolution at a meeting of the American Bar Association. I was honored to be paired with one of the world's foremost experts on mediation, John Wade from Bond University in Australia. I looked forward to learning about his approach to dispute resolution.

During his half of the session, Professor Wade described what he calls a "life goals analysis," which is a short list of one's personal and business goals, both short-term and long-term. Preparing this list is a useful tool for putting a dispute into perspective. He provided the following example (which is partially described in his paper "Systematic Risk Analysis for Negotiators and Litigators: How to Help Clients Make Better Decisions.")

A Chinese husband and his wife were negotiating a division of their property as part of a divorce. The husband had a large income and substantial assets. He was a prominent physician in the Chinese community and had many friends. The wife had little income and few assets. She felt isolated from their community.

The couple negotiated a split of their assets except for the last $40,000. During mediation, the wife completed a life goals analysis but the husband (perhaps buoyed by his community support) refused. In the end, they evenly split the $40,000.

After the divorce was finalized in court, the husband and his supporters left the courtroom and headed to a restaurant to celebrate. As the wife left the courtroom, she turned to the husband's attorney and said, "Now it is time to get even." She immediately went to a medical society office and filed a complaint against the doctor claiming that he had performed an illegal abortion on her and had illegally sent drugs to relatives in China. As a result, he lost his license to practice, his income and his prestige in the community.

If the physician had placed the dispute into the perspective of a life goals analysis, he might have gladly agreed to give the wife the entire $40,000 or more. His goals might have included continuing financial success, leadership in the medical community, developing a new personal relationship, and enjoying the fruits of his labors. Instead, he lost everything.

The moral of the story is this: Regardless of whether you are involved in a dispute resolution process or a deal making negotiation, try to take a "big picture" perspective and think of your immediate objectives in light of your life goals. I wish you the best of luck in this endeavor!

APPENDICES:

PLANNING CHECKLIST AND ASSESSMENT TOOL

A. Negotiation Planning Checklist
B. Example of a Completed Negotiation Planning Checklist
C. Assess Your Negotiating Style

Appendix A

Negotiation Planning Checklist

Use the following checklist when planning for negotiations.*
For background information, see Chapters 3, 5 and 6.

Goals and Best Alternatives

1. What is my goal in this negotiation? Why do I want to achieve this goal?

2. What is my best alternative for achieving this goal if this negotiation is not successful?

3. Will I disclose my best alternative to the other side during the negotiation? (Usually "yes" if your alternative is strong and "no" if your alternative is weak.)

4. How can I improve my best alternative? (By improving your alternative, you increase your power.)

5. What is the other side's goal in this negotiation? Why do I think the other side wants to achieve this goal? (At the planning stage, this is a guess.)

6. What is the other side's best alternative for achieving its goal if this negotiation is not successful? (Again, this is a guess.)

7. How can I weaken the other side's best alternative? (By weakening the other side's best alternative, you increase your power.)

Issues Likely to Arise (apart from price)

8. What issues are likely to arise during negotiations? List these issues and after each issue note:

   a. whether you think it is "tradable" because it is of low importance to you or "not tradable" because the issue is important to you,

   b. why the issue (if "not tradable") is important to you,

   c. facts you can use to support your position on each issue,

   d. whether the other side will think the issue is "tradable" or "not tradable" (at the planning stage, this is a guess), and

   e. why you think the issue is important to the other side (again, a guess).

   Use a spreadsheet when answering #8.

9. Do I have a personal or long-term relationship with the other side? If so, how might this affect my and the other side's stance on the issues? If not, how can I build a relationship with the other side?

10. Using the analysis at #8, what are the possible ways to create value for both sides—for example, by trading issues or by meeting interests? List questions you want to ask the other side when exploring these possibilities.

Questions Relating to Price

11. What is my reservation price? Why is this price important to me? (The reservation price is the lowest price you are willing to accept if you are the seller or the highest price you are willing to pay if you are the buyer.)

12. What is the most likely price? (This is a reasonable target price.)

13. What is my stretch goal? (Use this stretch early in negotiations. This is the highest price or the lowest price—depending on whether you are the seller or the buyer—that you can reasonably justify.)

14. Should I be the first to state a price? (Consider anchoring the other side to your offer by giving the first price when you are fairly confident about the value. If you are not confident about the value, asking the other side to make the offer is one way to determine value—but avoid becoming anchored to the other side's number.)

Authority When Agents Are Involved

15. Am I negotiating as an agent? If so, what are the limits of my authority?

16. If the other side is acting as an agent, what are the limits of the other side's authority? (This information should come from the principal, not the agent.)

*Thank you to the International Association for Contract & Commercial Management (IACCM) for encouragement in the development of this planner. IACCM, in partnership with Huthwaite International, produced a benchmark study entitled "Improving Corporate Negotiation Performance." The study notes the importance of planning to negotiation success but concluded that most companies do not use formal planning tools. After reviewing a planning template included in the study, I prepared a list of items that should be in a planner and presented them to contract professionals at IACCM conferences in the United States and Europe and during a webinar. This planning checklist incorporates feedback from these veteran negotiators.

Appendix B

Example of a Completed Negotiation Planning Checklist

This example of a completed planning checklist uses the following scenario from Chapter 3:

> You have decided to sell your car and are preparing to negotiate with a potential buyer, Kyle. Kyle is the only person who responded to your sales ad. You need at least $4,000 from the sale of the car to finance the purchase of a truck you have ordered. You want to keep your car for three more weeks, which is when the truck will arrive. The reasonable value of the car (based on several online calculators) is $5,000. If you can't find a buyer willing to pay at least $4,500, you will sell the car to your friend Terry for $4,000. You know that Terry will let you keep the car for the next three weeks.

Goals and Best Alternatives

1. What is my goal in this negotiation? Why do I want to achieve this goal?

   My goal is to sell my car. I want to sell the car so that I can finance the purchase of a truck that is on order.

2. What is my best alternative for achieving this goal if this

negotiation is not successful?

I will sell the car to my friend Terry for $4,000.

3. Will I disclose my best alternative to the other side during the negotiation? (Usually "yes" if your alternative is strong and "no" if your alternative is weak.)

   I will disclose that another buyer is interested but will not disclose the price, which is less than what I hope to receive from Kyle.

4. How can I improve my best alternative? (By improving your alternative, you increase your power.)

   I could try to find other buyers by placing more ads and by detailing the car.

5. What do I think is the other side's goal in this negotiation? Why do I think the other side wants to achieve this goal? (At the planning stage, this is a guess.)

   Kyle obviously wants to buy a car but at this point I don't know the reason for this goal.

6. What is the other side's best alternative for achieving its goal if this negotiation is not successful? (Again, this is a guess.)

   I assume that Kyle will buy a car from someone else.

7. How can I weaken the other side's best alternative? (By weakening the other side's best alternative, you increase your power.)

   I will attempt to show that Kyle won't get a better deal than what I am offering.

Issues Likely to Arise (apart from price)

8. What issues are likely to arise during negotiations? List these issues and after each issue note:

    a. whether you think it is "tradable" because it is low importance to you or "not tradable" because the issue is important to you,

    b. why the issue (if "not tradable") is important to you,

    c. facts you can use to support your position on each issue,

    d. whether the other side will think the issue is "tradable" or "not tradable" (at the planning stage, this is a guess), and

    e. why you think the issue is important to the other side (again, a guess).

    Use a spreadsheet when answering #8.

    In addition to price, analyzed at Questions 11-14, the main issue is the transfer date. (a) This is not tradable. (b) The transfer date is important to me because I need the car for transportation until my truck arrives. (c) I will explain how I use the car. (d) Uncertain at this time. (e) Uncertain at this time.

9. Do I have a personal or long-term relationship with the other side? If so, how might this affect my and the other side's stance on the issues? If not, how can I build a relationship with the other side?

    I have no relationship with Kyle. Because this is a one-time transaction, there is no need to build a relation-

ship apart from spending some time at the beginning of the negotiation getting to know Kyle.

There is a relationship with Terry (who is a friend), which is why I am willing to sell the car to Terry for a lower price.

10. Using the analysis at #8, what are the possible ways to create value for both sides—for example, by trading issues or by meeting interests? List questions you want to ask the other side when exploring these possibilities.

If the issue of transfer date is tradable by Kyle, I might be able to keep the car for three more weeks by lowering my price—but not below my reservation price.

If the transfer date is not tradable by either of us, I need to ask Kyle why that date is important. If Kyle needs the car for a specific reason over the next three weeks, when I also need the car, we might be able to work out an arrangement where one person gets the car but provides transportation to the other.

Questions Relating to Price

11. What is my reservation price? Why is this price important to me? (The reservation price is the lowest price you are willing to accept if you are the seller or the highest price you are willing to pay if you are the buyer.)

My reservation price is $4,500. I need at least $4,000 (which I can obtain from Terry) to purchase the truck.

12. What is the most likely price? (This is a reasonable target price.)

The most likely price is $5,000.

13. What is my stretch goal? (Use this stretch early in negotiations. This is the highest price or the lowest price—depending on whether you are the seller or the buyer—that you can reasonably justify.)

    My stretch goal is $6,000.

14. Should I be the first to state a price? (Consider anchoring the other side to your offer by giving the first price when you are fairly confident about the value. If you are not confident about the value, asking the other side to make the offer is one way to determine value—but avoid becoming anchored to the other side's number.)

    In this case, I am fairly confident about value, so I will open with my stretch goal of $6,000.

Authority When Agents Are Involved

15. Am I negotiating as an agent? If so, what are the limits of my authority?

    I am not negotiating as an agent.

16. If the other side is acting as an agent, what are the limits of the other side's authority? (This information should come from the principal, not the agent.)

    As far as I know, Kyle is not acting as an agent, but I should confirm this with Kyle. If Kyle is an agent, I will ask the principal about Kyle's authority.

Appendix C

Assess Your Negotiating Style

(See Chapter 2)

First, use the attachment to assess and understand your negotiating style.

Then use the assessment to assess the style of the other side. This is especially important in cross-cultural negotiations. Remember that there can be considerable variation in negotiation style within a culture.

Finally, do a gap analysis. Locate the major gaps between your style and the style of the other side.

After completing this assessment, you might try a role reversal exercise where you use the style of the other side. This will enable you to better understand the other side's style.

Thank you to Jeswald Salacuse, Henry J. Braker Professor of Law and former Dean of The Fletcher School at Tufts University, for permission to reprint this assessment, which is from his article "Ten Ways that Culture Affects Negotiating Style: Some Survey Results," *Negotiation Journal*, July 1998.

Assessing Your Negotiating Style

Instructions: Listed below are ten important traits of a person's negotiating style and approach. Each trait demonstrates a wide range of variations, which can be organized along a continuum, as has been done below. With respect to each trait, indicate with an X where your own negotiating style and approach in business negotiation falls along each continuum.

1. *Goal*: What is your goal in business negotiations: a binding contract or the creation of a relationship?

2. *Attitudes*: What is your attitude toward negotiation: win/lose or win/win?

3. *Personal Styles*: During negotiations, is your personal style informal or formal?

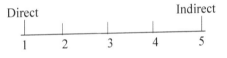

4. *Communications*: Is your communication style in negotiation direct (for instance, clear and definite proposals and answers) or indirect (for instance, vague, evasive answers)?

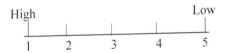

5. *Time Sensitivity*: In the negotiation process, is your sensitivity to time high (for instance, you want to make a deal quickly) or low (you negotiate slowly)?

6. *Emotionalism*: During negotiations, is your emotionalism high (that is, you have a tendency to display your emotions) or low (you hide your feelings)?

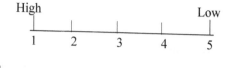

7. *Agreement Form*: Do you prefer agreements that are specific (that is, detailed) or general?

8. *Agreement Building*: Do you view negotiation as bottom up (reach agreement on details first) or top down (begin with agreement on general principle)?

9. *Team Organization*: As a member of a negotiating team, do you prefer having one leader who has authority to make a decision or decision making by consensus?

10. *Risk Taking*: Is your tendency to take risks during negotiations high (for instance, your opening offer to sell is extremely high) or low?